THE BATTLE

of

HUBBARDTON

The Rear Guard Action that Saved America

BRUCE M. VENTER

THE
History
PRESS

Published by The History Press
Charleston, SC 29403
www.historypress.net

First published 2015

Manufactured in the United States

ISBN 978.1.62619.325.3

Library of Congress Control Number: 2014956422

Notice: The information in this book is true and complete to the best of our knowledge. It is offered without guarantee on the part of the author or The History Press. The author and The History Press disclaim all liability in connection with the use of this book.

Dedicated to
Carl Fuller
Faithful steward of the Hubbardton Battlefield Site

CONTENTS

PREFACE

The battle of Hubbardton was the only Revolutionary War engagement fought in Vermont. It was also the first close-action, heavy fighting between a combined British and German expeditionary force and the American northern army during Lieutenant General John Burgoyne's campaign of 1777.[1]

Participants fought "in a thick wood, in the very style that the Americans think themselves superior to regular troops," a British diarist observed. Indeed, Hubbardton would be a bloody slugfest that tested the combat readiness of the Patriots and surprised not a few of their red-coated opponents. Another British participant honestly admitted that the fight at Hubbardton proved that "neither [the redcoats] were invincible, nor the Rebels all Poltroons." This comment must have been a difficult observation for a proud king's man to write in his journal.[2]

Since the mid-nineteenth century, numerous studies of the 1777 campaign have described the battle of Hubbardton, but only one book about this engagement has been written. Colonel John Williams's 1988 study entitled *The Battle of Hubbardton: The American Rebels Stem the Tide* was produced by the Vermont Division for Historic Preservation to reexamine previous unpublished works written on the battle. The battle of Hubbardton escaped the popular historical radar because it was not until the 1960s that the State of Vermont acquired significant battlefield land, along Sucker Brook and the Mount Independence–Hubbardton military road, from the Fuller family, who had worked a farm there. Not until 1970 did the state open a museum and visitor's center. The site is still home to Fuller family buildings, long since abandoned.[3]

However, much earlier Vermonters recognized the site's historical importance. Early in the 1800s, someone installed on the field a hand-lettered sign on a pole. The Hubbardton Battle Monument Association was founded in 1856. Three years later on the anniversary of the battle, a marble monument replaced the wooden sign. The monument stands as originally installed on the Castleton road near the visitor's center.

In 1937, sixty years after Vermonters and others celebrated the battle's centennial, state legislators established the Hubbardton Battlefield Commission, which began purchasing battlefield land. In 1947, the Board of Historic Sites took over the commission's role, and the battlefield officially became one of Vermont's state historic sites. A visitor's center was constructed in 1970, perhaps in anticipation of the country's bicentennial celebration of the American Revolution. In 1971, the Hubbardton battlefield site was listed in the National Register of Historic Places. With the publication of Williams's new study in 1988, the center's exhibits were updated in 1991.[4]

Williams's book remained the standard battlefield guide until it went out of print. Since the state had no plans to republish it, I decided that visitors should have a replacement to Williams's monograph. While I do not disagree with Colonel Williams's basic premise that Hubbardton was "a classic example of a rear guard action," I do challenge some of his tactical observations and other details. I also thought it was important to provide a historical context for the battle. By starting my narrative at Fort Ticonderoga—when Burgoyne forced St. Clair to evacuate the fort and the American encampment on Mount Independence—I have come to a different assessment of Simon Fraser's actions at Hubbardton. I think my interpretation of how Colonel Ebenezer Francis was killed differs significantly from Williams's version too. Whether or not the British grenadiers scaled Mount Zion is also tackled. Unlike Williams, I had the benefit of more recently published German primary sources that were not available to him in 1988. I hope readers find my account a worthy successor to Williams's solid work.

Barely two thousand men fought at Hubbardton, but we should not measure this engagement in terms of numbers. The battle's significance eclipses the size of the forces committed. This fiercely fought rear guard action may have lasted scant hours, but the valor of those hours saved the northern Continental army and, perhaps, the American cause.

ACKNOWLEDGEMENTS

Almost twenty years ago, I had the opportunity to visit the Hubbardton battlefield with my longtime friend and mentor in all things Civil War, Dr. Richard J. Sommers, senior historian (now retired) at the United States Army Education and Research Center in Carlisle, Pennsylvania. We climbed Mount Zion together to get a truly magnificent bird's-eye view of the battlefield terrain. Our visit engendered an interest in the battle that remains to this day. As I recall, Dick and I had a lively debate about how the battle was fought.

A few years later, I was again at Hubbardton with my good friends Bob O'Neill, Horace Mewborn and Bud Hall, all respected historians in the field of Civil War cavalry studies. Our discussions were much more animated than the first time I was at Hubbardton, as we debated how Seth Warner and Simon Fraser fought the battle. They defended Warner's handling of the action, while I criticized his leadership. Over the years, I have fondly recalled the time we spent arguing the merits of how Warner fought the battle. I have softened on Warner and probably become a little more critical of Fraser.

I'm grateful to Horace for obtaining a copy of a rare article on William Twiss for me. Bob gave me his copy of *Vermont History*, which included Ennis Duling's very insightful article on the shortcomings of Thomas Anburey's account of the battle of Hubbardton as a primary source. I am truly blessed to have such good friends.

Another one of those friends is Bill Welsch, president of the American Revolution Round Table of Richmond and an avid student of the

Revolutionary War. Bill was always ready to answer any questions I had during my research and writing of this book. Bill's extensive library of (sometimes obscure) sources was very helpful.

On my many visits to the Hubbardton Battlefield, the site manager, Carl Fuller, has always warmly greeted me and answered all my questions. Carl took his personal time one day last October to walk a good length of the Mount Independence–Hubbardton military road with me, sharing his own insights about the terrain gained from many years of living on the battlefield itself. I am most grateful to Carl and have dedicated this book to him.

Special thanks to Eric Schnitzer, chief historian at the Saratoga National Historical Park. Eric generously provided space for me to use the files and materials he has acquired over the years on the 1777 campaign. He also suggested some primary source material from the Journal of the Johannes Schwalm Association that supplemented my research on Hubbardton. Eric was most helpful in answering my questions relating to Simon Fraser and the Jäger.

At the outset of this project, John Quarstein—historian, author, duck hunter and tour guide extraordinaire—was instrumental in sending me to the right people at The History Press.

As always, Michael Dolan, senior editor at the Weider History Group, was willing to offer his editorial advice.

I could not have arranged the images in this book without the assistance of Catherine Southworth, who was a tech wizard when it came to such matters. Julie Krick designed excellent maps for this book, and Maureen Malone assisted with the author's photo.

My commissioning editor at The History Press, Katie Orlando, was very supportive and helpful throughout the entire publishing process. Katie made a special effort to make sure all my images met the required specifications.

Katie Stitely, project editor, was extremely helpful and understanding during the editing process.

Chris Fox, curator at the Fort Ticonderoga Museum, answered my request for a digital copy of the Wintersmith map for this book. I appreciate his extra effort to make it fit the publisher's specifications.

Dr. Michael Gabriel, history professor at Kutztown University, provided advice and the image of Seth Warner's statue, which saved me a trip to Bennington.

I would also like to extend my grateful appreciation to Brian Lindner—corporate historian with the National Life Group, Montpelier, Vermont—for his willingness to provide a digital copy of Roy H.

Heinrich's artwork of the battle of Hubbardton that appears on the cover of my book. Brian also suggested the Seth Warner illustration that appears on the back cover.

The librarians and staff at the Vermont Historical Society were most helpful and friendly during the time I spent researching the collections at that excellent facility. It was a pleasure working there.

I must mention two scholars who have passed away. Although I never met Colonel John Williams, it is appropriate that I acknowledge the debt I owe him for providing a solid foundation for my study of the battle of Hubbardton. Colonel Williams wrote a first-rate monograph on the battle, which gave me many insights and leads to follow in my research. I would also like to acknowledge the inspiration provided by Dr. Robert J. Christen, history professor at Manhattan College, who, many years ago, explained the importance of primary sources when writing history.

Our beagle, Sally, tramped the Hubbardton fields with me many times with her nose to the ground, sniffing out the truth of what happened on July 7, 1777. She always got excited when we approached this site, knowing there would be new things to find, as I did, too.

A special, heartfelt thank-you goes unconditionally to my wife, Lynne, who has supported all my history-related projects. She has walked many battlefields with me, including Hubbardton, and proofread more pages than can be counted. She has partnered with me in our tour and conference company and has added a special something to my life.

Lieutenant General John Burgoyne (1722–1792), by Joshua Reynolds, circa 1766. *Courtesy of the Frick Collection.*

INTRODUCTION

I have beat them!" King George III exclaimed to Queen Charlotte as he burst in on his half-dressed wife in her bedchamber. "I have beat all the Americans!"

The monarch's euphoria resulted from a dispatch the king had just received from Lieutenant General John Burgoyne. In the communiqué, Burgoyne announced that he had taken the mighty rebel fortress at Ticonderoga. The fort had fallen on July 6, 1777, with nary a shot being fired. The good news had not reached London until mid-September, traveling as it did by sea. King George had good reason for his elation—the Royal army had captured a valuable piece of military real estate—but the campaign of 1777 was far from over.[5]

By December, the king's demeanor would change markedly on receipt of another missive from Burgoyne in which the former cavalryman, noted playwright and member of Parliament now had to tell his sovereign that he had failed—and miserably. In October, the cocky fifty-five-year-old general, undone by a superior American force led by Major General Horatio Gates, had to surrender his entire army. While a devastating loss at the time, the extended consequences spelled doom for His Majesty's effort to squash the rebellion in his Atlantic coast colonies. Burgoyne's surrender at Saratoga, New York, on October 17, 1777, would mark a definitive turning point in the American War for Independence. The following March, France—Great Britain's arch-foe for a century—would ally with the rebellious colonies. The end result would be a Franco-American victory at Yorktown, nearly to the day of Burgoyne's surrender, four years later.

But neither defeat nor surrender was in the English air in the spring of 1777. That February, Burgoyne submitted a plan to the king and his secretary of state for the colonies, Lord George Germain, which seemed a surefire formula for success. British politicians and military men commonly held that the true font of colonial resistance was New England—perhaps more specifically, Massachusetts. After all, hadn't Massachusetts been the scene for a dozen years of insurgent uprisings like the Stamp Act riots, with its horrific tarring and feathering of Crown officials; the Boston Massacre; and the Boston Tea Party? Massachusetts Bay colonists had been front and center whenever agents of the mother country came under violence. The war itself had started with shots fired at British regulars at Lexington and Concord on April 19, 1775. Two months later, the bloody battle on Charlestown's Bunker Hill solidified the colonists' resolve to form an army with George Washington as its commander. If Great Britain isolated New England, as a physician might quarantine an infectious patient, conventional British wisdom held that the rebellion would fray and disintegrate for lack of a festering source. Burgoyne's strategic proposal to control the Hudson River in New York, cutting off New England's rebels from their counterparts in the middle and southern colonies, was a plan worthy of implementation.

Its author was not only a talented military man but also a wily politician. John Burgoyne had outmaneuvered several rival generals to get the king's ear. Of course, the three-pronged script he had written had him in the lead role. In the outline he circulated, Burgoyne freely personalized his scheme, referring to "my expedition" without knowing whether the king and his ministers would appoint him commander. Burgoyne offered to lead an army south from Canada, using the Lake Champlain–Lake George water corridor with the goal of capturing Albany, a town on the Hudson River's west bank. Burgoyne's putative force would include British regulars, German hirelings, Loyalists, some French Canadians, sailors, Indian allies and a "brilliant staff"—in total, 9,078 men. His train of artillery would include 138 guns of various sizes. It was an impressive force but not exactly what Burgoyne had in mind. As one historian has concluded, "The army [Burgoyne] met in May [1777] did not equal in strength the force that he had recommended, but its quality was beyond dispute."[6]

In tandem with Burgoyne's march southward, General Sir William Howe, the British commander in chief in the colonies, would march north from New York City, a port city Howe had taken from Washington the year before. Howe's march north to Albany was essential for Burgoyne's strategic plan to succeed. A third leg of Burgoyne's plan had a smaller force of redcoats,

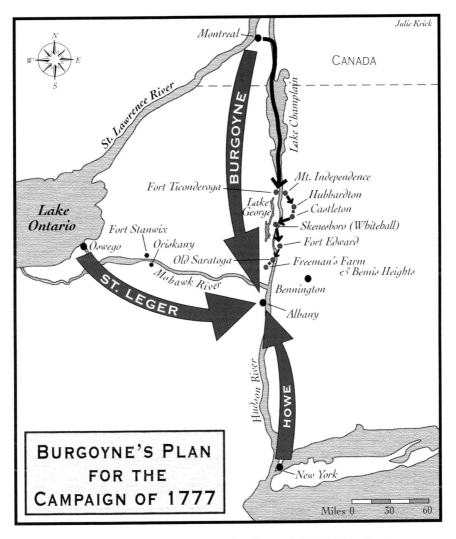

A map of Burgoyne's plan for the 1777 campaign. *Prepared by Julie Krick for the author.*

Loyalists and Indians under Lieutenant Colonel Barry St. Leger attack the Mohawk Valley from the west after landing on the shores of Lake Ontario. St. Leger first would capture Fort Schuyler (also known as Fort Stanwix) and then follow the Mohawk River to Albany. He would rendezvous with Burgoyne and Howe at Albany, giving the British control of the Hudson River. Burgoyne would bring the celebratory champagne, his favorite drink.[7]

Unfortunately for the British, not one subsequent event went according to Burgoyne's plan. Howe, bent on capturing Philadelphia where the upstart Continental Congress was meeting, decided on his own to chase after Washington, who would try to protect the capital. Howe reasoned that defeating Washington should now be a primary goal for Great Britain. Howe secured Lord Germain's approval to change the grand strategy for 1777, a decision Burgoyne only learned about after he arrived in Canada. It would not deter Burgoyne, however, from his goal to capture Albany.

A halfhearted attempt was made by Howe's subordinate, Major General Sir Henry Clinton, to invade the Hudson Valley in October 1777. Clinton's move was well after Burgoyne was stalled in heavy fighting with the American army near Saratoga, thirty miles north of his intended target. But Clinton's feeble effort, although he captured two American forts near West Point, proved to be too little and too late. Meanwhile, St. Leger had been stopped one hundred miles from Albany in August at Oriskany, a bloody slugfest that eventually caused him to abandon his siege of Fort Schuyler. The only prong in Burgoyne's triad plan that was emphatically pushed was his own, until he was defeated, surrounded and overwhelmed by an American force three times his army's size at Saratoga.

But could Burgoyne's invasion have succeeded? The answer may lie in a sometimes-overlooked battle fought early in the campaign. After capturing Fort Ticonderoga and Mount Independence, a wing of Burgoyne's army had the opportunity to defeat and perhaps capture a significant portion of the American northern army. But at Hubbardton, in the New Hampshire Grants (soon to be known as Vermont), the doggedness of fewer than one thousand Continentals under Colonel Seth Warner stopped the British pursuit of Major General Arthur St. Clair's fleeing army. Major Alexander Lindsay, the Earl of Balcarres and commander of ten light infantry companies in Burgoyne's army, later testified in specific regard to the Patriot prowess on display at Hubbardton. He said, "Circumstanced as the enemy was, as an army very hard pressed in their retreat, they certainly behaved with great gallantry."[8] British nobles rarely voiced such martial respect for the American rebels during the War of Independence.

Although Warner ignored St. Clair's orders, the Vermonter's decision might have been a good one. Warner's stubborn rear guard action so effectively kept Burgoyne's troops from pouncing on St. Clair's army that the retreating Patriots could rally at Fort Edward under their department commander, Major General Philip Schuyler, and fight another day. That day would come two months later near Saratoga, where Burgoyne's hopes and dreams of victory and glory would be shattered with an ignominious surrender to a former British army officer turned rebel named Horatio Gates.

Many of the men who faced the British and Germans two months later at Saratoga had fought their first pitched battle with the enemy at Hubbardton. Their presence at Saratoga in October 1777 may be attributed to an earlier, successful rear guard engagement fought at Hubbardton, which saved St. Clair's northern army and, as a result, might have saved the American cause.

"WHERE A GOAT CAN GO, A MAN CAN GO"

With the trained eye of an army engineer, Lieutenant William Twiss gazed over the terrain he saw atop Sugar Loaf Hill, later known as Mount Defiance. It was about two o'clock in the afternoon on July 5, 1777. American defenders had lost a grip on their outer lines around Fort Ticonderoga three days earlier. The thirty-two-year-old officer was accompanied by Major Griffith Williams, commander of Burgoyne's artillery corps, and Brigadier Simon Fraser, the latter using "an excellent compass" to guide the party up the hill. They joined Captain James Craig, forty light infantrymen and a handful of Indians who had been dispatched the day before by Fraser to occupy Sugar Loaf. Twiss had already garnered accolades from General Guy Carleton, the commander of British forces in Canada. Carleton reported that he recognized Twiss's "particular distinction" in the previous year's campaign. Now that British forces had gained access to the mountain, Twiss would have another opportunity to shine. It was an "abominably hot" summer day, Fraser later remembered, but the redcoat officers' arduous climb up the wooded slope yielded much promise for the British army facing Fort Ticonderoga.[9]

Twiss had been assigned as an aide to Major General William Phillips, in addition to his duties as chief engineer for Burgoyne's army, which had left Canada on June 16, bound for Albany. Phillips was second in command in Burgoyne's army. But more importantly, Phillips was an accomplished artillery officer who had gained fame during the Seven Years' War in

Modern-day view of Fort Ticonderoga taken from Mount Defiance. *Courtesy of Sandy Goss/ Eagle Bay Media.*

Europe. His handling of British guns at the 1760 battle of Warburg became a textbook example of how artillery could attack alongside cavalry. Twiss and Williams had been ordered to climb the 853-foot hill to see if it offered an opportunity for the placement of an artillery battery. Cannon atop the undefended position would dominate the American army's position at Fort Ticonderoga on the west side of Lake Champlain and at Mount Independence situated on the lake's east side. It would require a one-mile-long road cut for the guns, but the rewards were worth it, Twiss argued. Once a battery was in place, the Americans could not "make any material movement or preparation [during the day] without being discovered, and having their numbers counted," Burgoyne later reported.[10]

Possession of Sugar Loaf would put the American position well within the range of Burgoyne's twelve-pounders. To support Twiss's report of the advantages offered by Sugar Loaf's elevation, General Phillips allegedly claimed, "Where a goat can go, a man can go, and where a man can go, he can drag a gun [behind him.]" Whether Phillips actually uttered these now famous words, his biographer has concluded that this statement was "a precise reflection of Phillips' battlefield perspective" and "his personal philosophy." Phillips's gutsy

Major General Arthur St. Clair (1737–1818). *Courtesy of the National Archives, 148-CCD-43.*

leadership and the gritty determination of four hundred British foot soldiers paid off as two guns were manhandled up the hill within twenty-four hours.[11]

A logical question is: why wasn't Sugar Loaf fortified by the Americans to protect it from British seizure? The Ticonderoga promontory was a system of earthworks, redoubts and blockhouses, all constructed over a two-year period to tie together the old fort on the lake's west side with the newly fortified encampment across the lake. Montcalm's old French Lines from 1758 were incorporated into the scheme. But no works were ever built on the mountain that overlooked the La Chute River southwest of the fort. An American staff officer named John Trumbull had argued for a redoubt on top of the

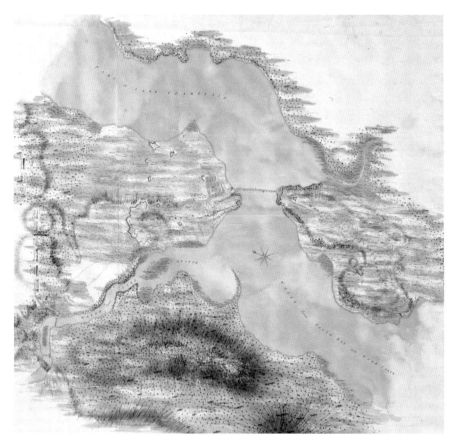

A map of Fort Ticonderoga and Mount Independence as surveyed by British assistant engineer Lieutenant Charles Wintersmith in 1777. This map shows the bridge across Lake Champlain connecting the two fortifications before St. Clair's evacuation on July 6, 1777. *Courtesy of the Fort Ticonderoga Museum Collection and Chris Fox, curator.*

mountain, but his commander at the time, Horatio Gates, rejected his young aide's proposal. Gates felt that to tie Sugar Loaf into the existing defensive plan would require more time, money and manpower than it was worth. But the major deterrent for a fortification on Sugar Loaf was water. There was no reasonable way to supply the isolated garrison with water, especially one under siege. Sugar Loaf went undefended, to Burgoyne's advantage.[12]

Three days prior to Twiss's excursion, Burgoyne had begun to disembark his army for an attack or, if need be, a siege of the American fortifications. At Three Mile Point north of Fort Ticonderoga, the redcoat contingent of Burgoyne's command, led by Brigadier Simon Fraser's Advance Corps along with some Loyalist scouts and Indian allies, was put ashore.[13] On the east side of Lake Champlain, Major General Friedrich Baron von Riedesel's German command, mostly soldiers hired from the principalities of Brunswick (Braunschweig) and Hesse-Hanau, was unloaded. Burgoyne's plan was to create a double envelopment of the American lines, with Fraser investing Fort Ticonderoga and Riedesel cutting off a Patriot retreat by crossing East Creek above Mount Independence. The thirty-nine-year-old German general, a veteran of the Seven Years' War, was expected to block the military road that led out of the eastside fortifications to the commonly called New Hampshire Grants (present-day Vermont). The name was shortened to the "Hampshire Grants" by settlers who moved there.[14] Burgoyne had masterminded a brilliant military strategy for capturing Fort Ticonderoga and destroying the enemy. However, like so many well-conceived military operations, its execution did not go as planned.

General Arthur St. Clair, the newly appointed American commander at Fort Ticonderoga and Mount Independence, watched Burgoyne's movements with great anticipation. St. Clair had only arrived at the rebel fortifications on June 13, three days before his adversary sailed from Canada. The Scotsman found the Ticonderoga works grossly undermanned and badly in need of repairs. On the Fort Ticonderoga side, the Patriots had improvised on remnants of the old French Lines west of the fort by adding some redoubts. The French Lines had been built nearly twenty years earlier when another fort commander, Marquis de Montcalm, had successfully defended Fort Carillon (Ticonderoga's previous name) against the British in 1758. On Mount Independence (formerly known as Rattlesnake Hill), the Americans had built a star-shaped fort with barracks inside, along with several blockhouses, a hospital and a large fortification called the Horse-Shoe Battery.

To connect the main fort and French Lines with the works on Mount Independence, a floating bridge supported by sunken wooden caissons had been constructed. To protect the bridge from enemy ships ascending Lake Champlain from the north, a chain and log boom was anchored above the bridge on either side of the lake. When St. Clair arrived at the promontory in June, much work still needed to be done to make the installation fit for military defense. The forty-year-old Scotsman immediately set fatigue details to work strengthening all parts of the terrain. Unfortunately, progress on the fortifications was painstakingly slow when alacrity was essential. Despite St. Clair's best efforts, the steps he would take and the decisions he would make would be roundly criticized, resulting in a formal court-martial a year later.

Early in the War for Independence, Fort Ticonderoga had been captured by a surprise attack jointly led by Benedict Arnold and Ethan Allen and his Green Mountain Boys. In May 1775, the lightly guarded British post was a valuable prize for the Continental Congress. Several months later, the Congress's newly appointed army commander, George Washington, soon saw value in the old fort, a relic of the French and Indian War, along with its sister fort at Crown Point. It was the two forts' contents, not their strategic locations, that appealed to the Virginian at the time.

During the siege of Boston—which had followed clashes at Lexington, Concord and Bunker Hill—New England militia regiments under Washington's command had bottled up the British army in the Massachusetts town. Among the redcoat generals stationed in Boston at the time were three men who would play major roles in the 1777 campaign two years later: John Burgoyne, William Howe and Henry Clinton. It's fair to say that Burgoyne's observation of the battle of Bunker Hill from Boston's Copp's Hill probably influenced his later decision to mount guns on Mount Defiance first, rather than risk an immediate frontal assault on St. Clair's works at Ticonderoga.

Six months after the capture of Fort Ticonderoga, Washington seized the opportunity presented by the captured contents of the fort. The forty-three-year-old general ordered his chief artillery officer, Colonel Henry Knox, to deliver as many cannon as he could haul from the Lake Champlain forts down to Albany and then over the Berkshire Mountains in western Massachusetts to Boston. It was an arduous assignment, but the competent, rotund Knox carried out his orders flawlessly. Some fifty-nine guns and mortars were delivered to Washington. Once the cannon were mounted on Dorchester Heights overlooking Boston Harbor, the British army was forced out of the city on March 17, 1776.

The Americans would hold Fort Ticonderoga from its capture in May 1775 until Burgoyne approached the fortress in June 1777. Patriot forces were lucky in October 1776 when British major general Guy Carleton's invading army was stalled at Lake Champlain's Valcour Island by the plucky leadership of a former merchant sea captain turned army officer named Benedict Arnold. Although defeated by Carleton in a pounding naval engagement, Arnold's dogged tactics delayed the British invasion long enough into the autumn months that Carleton was forced to rethink his campaign options. Despite urging from his subordinate commander, John Burgoyne, to continue the campaign, New York's approaching winter made further action unfeasible in Carleton's mind. The future Lord Dorchester retreated down the lake back to Canada; Fort Ticonderoga was safe for another season. As one historian has concluded, "Had Ticonderoga been taken [by Carleton] and held that coming winter, Burgoyne's campaign of 1777, starting from that point, would have almost certainly succeeded."[15]

The intervening months at Fort Ticonderoga after Carleton withdrew were mostly peaceful for the garrison and its commanders. Food and tent shortages, disease and frigid weather sapped the men more than gunfire. A soldier was more likely to freeze to death than die of a gunshot. The fort's commander during the winter months, Colonel Anthony Wayne, lamented the number of men in the ranks who were daily falling from fever, "camp distemper" and other maladies. At a post that General Schuyler claimed needed 10,000 soldiers to defend it properly, Wayne could barely muster 1,600 Continentals,

Brigadier Simon Fraser (1729–1777). *Courtesy of the Guttenberg Project.*

supplemented by a few hundred New England militiamen. When the Pennsylvania officer was promoted to brigadier general and ordered to join Washington's army in April 1777, he tried to put a good face on his former command. Wayne inaccurately reported to Washington that "all was well" and that the fort "can never be carried, without much loss of blood."[16]

Wayne's opinion might have influenced Washington's belief in Fort Ticonderoga's impregnability when he was considering dispatches from Schuyler in June 1777. Despite Wayne's optimism, it was a miserable situation that St. Clair walked into two months later. St. Clair later wrote, "Had every man I had, been disposed in single file on the different works and along the lines of defence [*sic*], they would have been scarcely within the reach of each other's voices."[17]

A month after Wayne penned his misleading report to Washington, things were racing forward at British headquarters in Quebec. The campaign of 1777 would see Burgoyne, who was more aggressive than the cautious Carleton, leading troops. The man calling the shots in London, George Germain, hated Carleton; the feeling was mutual. Carleton would remain in Canada as governor, while his former subordinate sailed south with grand fanfare. Now, in July 1777, the mighty fortress that some would call the key to the continent was in Burgoyne's sights, a prize that had eluded his commander the previous year.

With regimental bands playing, drums beating and flags flying, Burgoyne simultaneously landed the two wings of his army at Three Mile Point and north of East Creek. Investment operations against Fort Ticonderoga and Mount Independence had begun. His general orders the previous day reflected the pomp and circumstance of the occasion. He wrote, "We are to contend for the King, and the constitution of Great Britain, to vindicate Law, and to relieve the oppressed—a cause in which his Majesty's Troops and those of the Princes his Allies, will feel equal excitement." Adding the zest of an acclaimed author, the general continued, "The Services required of this particular expedition, are critical and conspicuous. During our progress occasions may occur, in which, nor difficulty, nor labour nor Life, are to be regarded." Finally, Burgoyne haughtily stated, "This Army must not Retreat." He would hold steadfastly to this caveat until all hope was lost three and a half months later.[18]

Brigadier Simon Fraser made short work of the anemic American defenses outside the French Lines. The forty-eight-year-old Scotsman was a career officer and veteran of the French and Indian War in America who commanded Burgoyne's Advance Corps, a highly specialized unit of shock troops. As preparations were underway for the upcoming campaign, there was an army rumor that if Fraser did a good job with his assignment, he would be made Earl of Lovat. This honor would restore his family's confiscated lands, lost when a previous earl had backed Bonnie Prince Charlie in the Scottish rebellion of 1745. An experienced combat commander, Fraser had developed a close personal friendship with Burgoyne during their previous year in Canada. Fraser served in the present campaign at the commanding general's personal request. Burgoyne was happy to praise his brigadier to Lord Germain, writing of Fraser's "uniform intelligence, activity, and bravery which distinguish his character on all occasions, and entitle him to be recommended in the most particular manner to his Majesty's notice." The feelings were mutual. Fraser considered his commander "a fine agreeable manly fellow." Burgoyne was also thought to have said that Fraser never begrudged "a danger or care in other hands than his own"—a prescient remark that would be fulfilled on the morning of July 7, 1777.[19] Fraser was the right man to command such a nonpareil unit.

The Advance Corps was made up of a grenadier battalion, the physically largest and most rugged men in each regiment; a battalion of light infantry, consisting of each regiment's most agile and fittest fighters; and eight companies of Fraser's own Twenty-fourth Foot, a so-called hat battalion. In the eighteenth century, British army grenadiers wore high mitered helmets to increase their height appearance, the light infantry had leather caps and the regular companies were accoutered with the traditional tricorn hat. Fraser was lieutenant colonel of the Twenty-fourth Foot, effectively the field commander of the regiment, except for this campaign, when he was promoted to brigadier. The hat companies, a term used to describe the line or battalion companies of a regiment and to distinguish them from grenadier and light infantry companies, were commanded by Major Robert Grant. Grant had held his majority in the regiment for only two years.[20]

During this period, a typical British regiment was composed of ten companies: one grenadier company, one light infantry company and eight battalion, or hat, companies. When an army went on active campaign, all the grenadier companies from the army's various regiments were put together to form a grenadier battalion. Likewise, all light infantry companies were formed into a battalion as well. This configuration made up the core of Fraser's Advance Corps.[21] Also attached to Fraser's corps were Indian allies and Captain Alexander Fraser's Company of Select Marksmen, who acted as scouts for the Advance Corps. Alexander was the brigadier's nephew. Simon Fraser's command was an elite fighting force that would be called upon many times by Burgoyne in desperate situations during the campaign. Serving as a detached reserve for the Advance Corps was Lieutenant Colonel Heinrich Breymann's corps of grenadiers, light infantry and a Jäger company.

On July 2, General Phillips ordered the Advance Corps forward. With Alexander Fraser's company and some Indians out in front, Simon Fraser's men easily captured Mount Hope, an already burning fortification that commanded a sawmill and the portage road to the landing at the northern end of Lake George. A few drunken Indians who came too close to St. Clair's defenses were the majority of the casualties suffered during the maneuver. British troops were now 1,400 yards from the Patriot lines, forming an undisputed arc around the thinly held former French Lines. American access to Fort George at the southern shore of Lake George was now cut off. Three days later, Lieutenant Twiss gained free access to Sugar Loaf Hill.[22]

Meanwhile, on July 1, General Riedesel's German regiments—excluding Breymann's command, which was with Fraser, and Lieutenant Colonel Friedrich von Baum's Prinz Ludwig Dragoons, which were attached to Burgoyne's headquarters—embarked on the east shore of Lake Champlain. The Germans cleared land for their camp as they awaited further orders. Burgoyne was anxious to cut off the Americans from a retreat via the Hampshire Grants, so he dispatched Captain Fraser's Select Marksmen, some Indians and Canadians on a far sweep around the army's left. Two days later, Riedesel's troops moved to surround the rebel post on Mount Independence

The 1776 military road as it approaches Mount Independence from the east. This modern-day view reflects a close resemblance to what the road would have looked like in 1777 to both American and British troops. *Courtesy of Lynne Venter.*

by cutting off the military road that had been built the previous year. If the Brunswickers successfully surrounded Mount Independence, it would give them firepower on the lake's shoreline south of the fort, a water escape route still open to the Patriots that led to Skenesborough, a small community at the southern end of Lake Champlain. Skenesborough (present-day Whitehall, New York) was named for Philip Skene, a Loyalist whose eighteenth-century version of urban development included tenant houses, a sawmill, a gristmill, storehouses, a foundry, a shipyard, a blockhouse and a large house for himself.[23]

Simon Fraser objected to using the Germans to block the American escape route from Mount Independence. He considered Riedesel's men "a helpless kind of troops in the woods, and a morass obliged the Corps to make a circuit of sixteen miles." In his latter observation, the brigadier was right. Fraser instead suggested that he be allowed to reconnoiter the east side of the American camp himself to see if he could find any advantageous ground to exploit against the rebels. Phillips opposed the move, insisting that

28

Burgoyne's army concentrate against the fort's defenses. In fact, Riedesel's Brunswickers found East Creek more difficult to ford than anticipated, and swamps to the east were equally problematic for his infantry to cross. It was a terrain feature that would prove providential for St. Clair's bedraggled army. Riedesel's failure to surround Mount Independence would allow the Patriots the option of using the military road to exit their fortifications.[24]

The Mount Independence–Hubbardton military road was hardly a highway but more a rutted trail that led to Castleton in the Hampshire Grants. The road eventually ended at the Fort at No. 4 in Charlestown, New

Major General Philip Schuyler (1733–1804). *Courtesy of the Library of Congress, LC-USZ62-45170.*

Hampshire. Sections of the older Crown Point military road, another relic of the French and Indian War, were incorporated into the American army's road system by order of General Gates while he commanded at Fort Ticonderoga. Although Fraser described the Mount Independence military thoroughfare, perhaps sarcastically, as a "great military road built by the rebels," one historian has more accurately characterized it as "but a pretense of a road…a mere wagon track, new, rough, rutted, and spotted with stumps of trees."[25]

The chief reason for building a military road in 1776 from the Hampshire Grants was because Mount Independence had become a major post in the northern theater of operations for the Patriots. Following the American retreat from Canada in 1776, two Patriots—Colonel Jeduthan Baldwin and Lieutenant Colonel John Trumbull—investigated high ground called Rattlesnake Hill, a quarter mile across the lake from Fort Ticonderoga. The two officers concluded it was more defensible than the fort's terrain and had a better water source. Trumbull and Baldwin convinced Schuyler and Gates the new area was ideally suited to build fortifications. Their observations were accepted; Rattlesnake Hill became known as Mount Independence in July 1776. Thousands of soldiers would march back and forth between

New York and New England using the military road, depending on the season or campaign activities. Tons of supplies were hauled over the road by ox-drawn carts or packhorses along with fresh meat on the hoof. It was a well-worn, if rough, path that kept the twin peninsulas of Ticonderoga and Mount Independence supplied until Burgoyne's army arrived. It would be one of two possible avenues of escape for General St. Clair's outnumbered command in the early morning hours of July 6, 1777.[26]

St. Clair and his staff began constantly monitoring British movements around the Ticonderoga promontory once the fifes and drums of redcoat regiments were heard on July 1. The new post commander later claimed in his court-martial that it had been hard to gauge Burgoyne's progress up Lake Champlain any sooner because every time St. Clair would order out scouting parties, they would be attacked by Indians and Tories. It became a dangerous business providing information to the general's headquarters at the fort. St. Clair was even reluctant to send the famed Whitcomb Rangers far from American lines. Some of St. Clair's best information came from British deserters. This intelligence would help determine St. Clair's next move—a decision his commander, Philip Schuyler, would agree with, but one that would put him in hot water with the Continental Congress.[27]

As department commander, Schuyler was well aware of the dismal condition of the works around Fort Ticonderoga and Mount Independence. He also knew that 10,000 men were needed to mount a proper defense against a British invasion. On St. Clair's first day on the job, he wrote his commander apprising him of the dire situation, claiming he only had 1,576 soldiers fit for duty. By June 28, St. Clair would have 500 more rank and files ready to fight, but this was hardly reassuring to the desperate commander. To reassure the fort's new commandant that he had his support, Schuyler personally journeyed from his headquarters at Fort Edward to Fort Ticonderoga, where he met with St. Clair and three of his general officers on June 20. This council of war outlined the problems facing St. Clair, his options and Schuyler's endorsement of an exit strategy.[28]

Schuyler also kept his commander in chief, George Washington, informed of the northern department's situation through myriad correspondence during the month of June and into July. It was well understood that Congress valued the Ticonderoga post, probably much beyond its actual strategic worth. Washington, who had never visited the fort or Mount Independence up to that point in the war, shared the politicians' viewpoint on its importance. If it became necessary for St. Clair to abandon his post, Congress would obviously expect heads to roll.[29]

EVACUATION

Once Simon Fraser captured Mount Hope on July 4, less than a year after the Declaration of Independence had been read on the parade ground at Mount Independence, Arthur St. Clair started making decisions. His dilemma—whether to hold his post to the last extremity or abandon it and save the army—weighed heavily on his mind. His only aide de camp, Major Isaac Dunn, later claimed the general slept only "one hour in four and twenty, on an average, till the evacuation took place." During every alarm, St. Clair "always appeared on the lines, going from right to left encouraging the troops, putting them in mind of the cause they were engaged in, [and] telling them to keep themselves cool." In a tight situation, the Scotsman showed no lack of courage.[30]

With portage access to Lake George now blocked, the post commander needed to think quickly. Up to this time, St. Clair had done little to prepare for the evacuation, except for sending his eleven-year-old son to Fort George on June 29. It was the general's opinion that he should wait until the last possible minute to abandon the fort and his army's main encampment across the lake. He knew the value Congress placed on the fort and its environs. But he also knew his position was becoming more untenable each day. It may be too harsh a term to say St. Clair dithered while Burgoyne gobbled up real estate around him. While he showed no lack of bravery as a commander, his languid behavior in this crisis would cost the American army dearly in terms of foodstuffs, ammunition, arms and cannon left to British.[31]

About noontime on July 5, a Patriot captain "spy'd a party of the British troops on the Mountains which overlooks Ti."[32] Once redcoat light infantrymen were spotted on top of Sugar Loaf, St. Clair decided to act. He knew instinctively that troops on the hill would spell disaster for his position. If the British managed to haul cannon up the slope, they could easily dominate the fort and Mount Independence with plunging artillery fire. And that is exactly what Lieutenant Twiss and his superiors had in mind.

The Indians who accompanied Captain Craig to the summit were no help to British plans. Phillips and Burgoyne wanted to keep their intentions for Sugar Loaf a secret as long as possible. Whether it was Craig's carelessness or his inability to control the savages, nevertheless, campfire smoke was detected arising from the summit of the mountain, an occurrence not lost on American defenders. Notwithstanding the smoking campfires, the noise of pioneer crews building a trail and hauling cannon up the slope would have been evident in a frontier region nearly devoid of ambient noise.

While the surprise of seeing twelve-pounder barrels ominously facing the fort was now lost, the anticipation was not. One British officer told his journal that once the smoke was seen by the rebels, "all their pretended boastings of holding out to the last, and choosing rather to die in their works than give them up, failed them."[33]

Surely St. Clair was aware of the ramifications of a British battery on Sugar Loaf Hill. Twenty years earlier, Montcalm had questioned the wisdom of building Fort Carillon so near to Sugar Loaf. John Trumbull, who served as deputy adjutant general under General Gates, also posited that cannon placed on Sugar Loaf could dominate Fort Ticonderoga and the newly christened Mount Independence. While some officers chided the Harvard graduate for his perceived naiveté, a kindly Gates allowed the young officer to test his thesis. Trumbull had artillery aimed from both the fort and a battery across the lake. Shots from both sites hit near the summit of Sugar Loaf, proving the young officer's point. To see if guns could be manhandled up the mountain, he hiked it along with Anthony Wayne and Benedict Arnold, who were at the fort at the time. Again, all agreed, cannon could be hauled to the top of Sugar Loaf. Whether Wayne shared the insight gained from his trek with Trumbull with St. Clair is unrecorded, but chances are some officer mentioned it, especially when Burgoyne's battalions disembarked at Three Mill Point.[34]

Whether two field pieces perched on Sugar Loaf put the American army in imminent danger is a matter of speculation. The more immediate threat to St. Clair's position was Riedesel's maneuver to outflank Mount Independence by crossing East Creek, which would put German troops on the military road in his rear. This road represented one of only two escape routes for the Patriot army at this point. The military road to Hubbardton offered the only practical option for getting two thousand plus men off the mount.

St. Clair acted quickly. He convened a council of general officers to consider what to do next. Present at the meeting were Brigadier Generals Matthias Roche de Fermoy, Enoch Poor and James Patterson, along with Colonel Pierce Long. Long was included because he would command the water-bound retreat the next morning. St. Clair suggested that "there was every reason to believe that the batteries of the enemy are ready to open up upon the Ticonderoga side," and the Patriot defenses would be "enfiladed on all quarters." Furthermore, he stated that troop returns showed only 2,089 Continental effectives were available, along with 900 militiamen expected only to stay a few more days. The commanding officer then asked his subordinates for their opinion. The war council was unanimous in its decision: it was impossible with the available troops to defend Ticonderoga and Mount Independence. All soldiers, artillery and stores should be removed that night to Mount Independence.[35]

In hindsight, however, the extraordinary ability to point two twelve-pounders, with more cannon to follow, at the American lines on July 6 was meaningless in the grand scheme of the campaign. Less than two hundred miles south of Fort Ticonderoga, in New York City, on July 5, Burgoyne's fate (rather than St. Clair's) was sealed. General Howe had loaded his army on transports bound for Philadelphia and a showdown with Washington. Howe would not come up the Hudson River to Albany as expected in Burgoyne's plan approved in London the previous February. There would be no champagne toast in Albany.

In addition, Howe refused to consider arguments made by his second in command, Sir Henry Clinton. Clinton felt that a conjunction with Burgoyne was the right way to go. The option was open as long as Howe's troops sat on their crowded transports in New York Harbor. Once Howe heard on July 23 that Fort Ticonderoga had fallen, however, he ordered the ships to weigh anchor and sail for the Chesapeake Bay. Clinton's points were indeed valid: Washington would be free to send reinforcements to the northern department if Howe abandoned the Hudson. Burgoyne would desperately need a supply line from the Hudson rather than the long haul from Canada. Moving British ships up the river would push the rebels out of their highland forts near West Point. Howe considered Clinton's big-picture strategy lesson valid but decided that Burgoyne could fend for himself, a selfish position that would become evident three months later, despite the successful capture of Philadelphia.[36]

About three o'clock in the morning on July 6, two rebel deserters approached the outer picket line of Fraser's Advance Corps. They eagerly reported that St. Clair had abandoned both Fort Ticonderoga and Mount Independence. At first, Fraser deemed the intelligence a ruse, calculated to draw his redcoats forward and then blast them with grapeshot. Campfires along the American lines had been kept blazing as a diversion, fooling a German surgeon into thinking that "houses and cottages were burning" near the fort. Fraser notified Burgoyne that something was up and then ordered his brigade to be ready to move, cautioning his men to hold down the noise.

Accompanied by Lieutenant Twiss and a small detachment of light infantrymen from the Ninth Foot, Fraser personally led them forward at daybreak. The brigadier's suspicions proved false when he found the rebel works empty. Fraser acted immediately to take possession of the fort. To his surprise, the Patriots had left vast quantities of ammunition, artillery pieces and provisions behind them. The only infrastructure they tried to destroy was the planking on the footbridge that connected the fort with the encampment on Mount Independence. Some of the planking had been removed and the rest set ablaze. Splashing lake water "quenched" the burning cross beams while Fraser quickly had the bridge's missing boards replaced. In no time, the regimental colors of the Ninth Foot were flying over the old French fort and the King's flag was waving proudly on Mount Independence.[37]

The rebels, however, had made good their escape. No fires were permitted, but lots of pushing and shoving occurred among a throng of angry and frightened men. St. Clair put the watercourse column under the charge of Colonel Long, whom the general valued as "an active, diligent, good officer." Long's responsibility was to take five armed galleys, two hundred bateaux and sundry other vessels loaded with every conceivable military store possible up Lake Champlain to Skenesborough. Women, sick soldiers unable to walk and six hundred troops packed boats loaded with provisions, cannon, tents, gunpowder, medical stores and baggage of all kind, including the garrison's pay chest. It was a motley crowd that set sail about 3:00 a.m. The wind kicked up as the Patriots departed, creating a chop that made the journey a nightmare for the invalids on board. The New Hampshire colonel would shepherd his flotilla through the "Drowned Land" of southern Lake Champlain without incident. Long's fleet arrived about 1:00 p.m. at Skenesborough, where his human cargo disembarked immediately. Unfortunately for St. Clair and the northern army, Long neglected to unload his valuable supplies, an error that showed his commander's praise misplaced.[38]

Modern-day view of Mount Independence taken from Mount Defiance. *Courtesy of Lynne Venter.*

While Long's makeshift navy sailed south to Skenesborough, the majority of St. Clair's command exited Mount Independence in darkness down the military road leading to Hubbardton. At three o'clock in the morning, the Patriot column began to move with Brigadier General Enoch Poor's New Hampshire brigade in the lead, followed by Patterson's Massachusetts brigade and Roche de Fermoy's mixed brigade of Green Mountain and Massachusetts Continentals and New Hampshire and Massachusetts militia. An hour later, companies from Colonel Ebenezer Francis's Eleventh Massachusetts Regiment brought up the rear. The retreat was far from orderly. St. Clair was forced to ride to the front of the column to restore order to the rank and file. He then returned to the column's rear, infuriated that Fermoy, contrary to orders, had set fire to his hut, which "lighted the whole Mount." But Fermoy's ineptitude was not an isolated problem for St. Clair.[39] Rebel deserters and panic-stricken militiamen firing muskets gave more than enough notice to the enemy that the key to the continent was lost.

One oft-repeated story about the Patriot retreat should be treated with a fair amount of skepticism. According to a memoir written in 1789 by Thomas Anburey, a British volunteer with the Twenty-ninth Foot's grenadier company, the redcoats who crossed the floating bridge to Mount Independence were supposed to be blasted to hell by a rebel cannon stationed at the end of the bridge. Anburey claimed when the British approached the mount, four cannoneers with lighted linstocks were found. Fortunately for Fraser's men, they were sprawled on the ground dead drunk with an empty keg of Madeira by their side. Undoubtedly, there were drunken rebels on the mount, according to American records, but not at the bridgehead. Anburey's tale has been repeated in several well-respected narratives of Burgoyne's campaign, but recent scholarship claims Anburey was a prolific plagiarist and downright made things up. A more credible account comes from the pen of Lieutenant William Digby, who observed that there was no gun at the end of the bridge. Digby posited that "had they placed one gun, so as the grape shot [could] take range on the bridge—and which surprised us they did not, as two men could have fired it, and then made off—they would, in all probability, have destroyed all or most of us on the Boom." With Digby's journal providing a more reliable account, Anburey's musings on the Patriot retreat and subsequent battle at Hubbardton must be treated more as myths than historical fact.[40]

But there were problems with St. Clair's retreat other than the whimsical drunks on Mount Independence. A soldier in Colonel Cilley's First New Hampshire Regiment found the withdrawal disheartening. "Such a Retreat was never heard of since the Creation of the world." At five o'clock in the afternoon on July 5, this man was ordered to draw forty-eight rounds of ammunition and nine days provisions, but all his Continental clothing was abandoned. What started out as a high-spirited march quickly disintegrated into a fatiguing, disorderly retreat as the army was trying to outrun the pursuing British regulars.[41]

Fraser's initial success in capturing Mount Independence was short-lived.[42] Once they reached the deserted encampment, his redcoats went wild, plundering the abandoned stores with "horrid irregularities." A German officer said that the rebels "had left their bakeries and breweries intact and a goodly supply of flour and beverages was found in both." A surgeon in Riedesel's corps claimed in his journal that it was "beyond description how much the enemy left behind in ammunition, provisions and such victuals as wine, rum, sugar, coffee, chocolate, butter, cheese, etc." From this delectable enumeration, it is easy to see why the redcoats went a little crazy on the mount. A chaplain in the Hessen-Hannau regiment recorded in that unit's journal that the Patriot cannon were only lightly spiked, and warehouses were left "full of food and drink. Many hundred oxen and sheep were walking around" the mount. The herd stock was distributed to the British, the Germans received only coffee and the Indians were awarded a supply of lead and powder. It was 5:00 a.m. before

A modern-day view looking east on the Mount Independence–Hubbardton military road. *Courtesy of Lynne Venter.*

Fraser's officers got his soldiers back under control. At that point, Fraser sent a message to Burgoyne that he was heading after the rebels, whom he judged to be four miles in front of him.[43]

3

PURSUIT

Once Burgoyne heard from Fraser that St. Clair was on the move, he ordered the British fleet to weigh anchor. Onboard the *Royal George*, the ship he used as his nightly headquarters, the British commander made plans to follow the rebel flotilla himself. Burgoyne had no problem allowing Fraser to pursue the Americans who were retreating over the Mount Independence–Hubbardton military road because the general knew with confidence "the safety I cou'd trust to that Officer's conduct." Instead, Burgoyne devoted his energy to breaking the boom that was supposed to stall enemy progress up the lake and following Long's disheveled armada.[44]

To break the boom and footbridge, Burgoyne turned to his fleet commander, Commodore Skeffington Ludwig. By the spring of 1777, the bridge and boom had been rebuilt after the original design had fallen victim to the lake's strong currents and winter ice flows. Twenty-two piers, built from hand-hewed timbers three to four feet thick and twenty-five feet long, were made into squares, chained together and filled with heavy rocks. A twelve-foot-wide floating bridge was attached with chains to the piers at distances of fifty feet each. To protect the floating bridge and stop enemy invaders, a heavy double-chained and round log boom was laid across the lake a few hundred feet north of the bridge.[45]

On Ludwig's command, his gunboats were moved forward. A few well-aimed cannonballs broke the boom and cut one fifty-foot section of the floating bridge, all to the "general animation" and cheering of the naval officers and seamen charged with the task. In a half hour, Burgoyne's frigates—the *Royal George* and *Inflexible*—gunboats and transports were plying the waters south of the fort. Onboard were hat or battalion companies of the Ninth, Twentieth and Twenty-first Foot. Meanwhile, Breymann's Corps had been transferred back to Riedesel on the east side of the lake. With the rebels on the run in two directions, Burgoyne had a right to feel pretty good about his accomplishments. In the haughty tone of an aspiring English aristocrat, he reported a few days later to London that his warships had sailed through "impediments which the Enemy had been labouring for months together to make impenetrable."[46] As the conqueror of Ticonderoga, he was entitled to crow, at least for a few days.

"Knowing the safety I cou'd trust to [Fraser's] conduct, I turned my chief attention to the pursuit by Water," Burgoyne wrote to Germain, "by which route I had Intelligence one Column were retiring in two hundred and twenty Batteaux [*sic*] covered by five armed Gallies [*sic*]." Burgoyne's scouts had given the general good information, and he would capitalize on it. With the boom and floating bridge no longer an impediment, by 10:00 a.m. on July 6, his frigates got underway in a chase up Lake Champlain. The Sixty-second Foot and the Prinz Frederic Regiment from Riedesel's corps were left at Fort Ticonderoga and Mount Independence to secure the stores captured by Fraser's quick action earlier that morning.[47]

It was three o'clock in the afternoon when the lead elements of Burgoyne's fleet arrived at South Bay about three miles north of Skenesborough. Companies of the Ninth, Twentieth and Twenty-first Foot disembarked for a flanking attack on the town. The frigates *Royal George* and *Inflexible*, along with the gunboats, continued sailing to Skenesborough Harbor. Leading the way with gunboats was an aggressive Captain John Carter of the Royal Artillery who trained his cannon on the American vessels riding in the harbor. Two of the American ships, the galley *Trumbull* and the schooner *Liberty*, immediately struck their colors. The sloop *Revenge* and the galley *Gates*, both loaded with gunpowder, were blown up, while the cutter *Enterprise* was set afire. Another gondola, the *New York*, also was sunk. The Patriots set fire to the stockade, mills, storehouses, bateaux and any piled-up supplies sitting on the docks. Although the Americans had done a good job moving large quantities of supplies from Fort Ticonderoga the previous night, despite a hasty evacuation, a year's worth of war materiel was lost in a matter of hours. No naval defense was made by the American flotilla prior to its arrival at Skenesborough. A British artillery officer told his journal that the southern end of Lake Champlain was "so narrow in some places that the Ships Yards almost touched the Precipices which over hung them." This man believed the rebels could have used these terrain features to

Modern-day view of Skenesborough Harbor (present-day Whitehall, New York), where Colonel Pierce Long's fleet was docked when it was attacked by Burgoyne's forces. *Author's collection*.

their advantage "by leaving a Detachment on the shore to harass" the British ships and gunboats. But a frazzled Colonel Long failed to act. Now on land with Skenesborough Harbor in flames, the men of Long's retreating column carried only the packs on their backs and the muskets in their hands.[48]

Things were happier in the British and German camps at Skenesborough after the Americans left. There seems to have been a goodly amount of rebel booty saved from the ashes. A German officer recorded in his journal that "the Savages and sailors nevertheless rescued so many tents, shirts, pieces of clothing and other items that they held a kind of country fair with them the next day."[49]

Opposite, top: New York state historic marker indicating where General Burgoyne defeated Colonel Pierce Long's retreating fleet at Skenesborough (present-day Whitehall, New York). *Courtesy of Lynne Venter*.

Opposite, bottom: Vermont state historic marker indicating a location on the Mount Independence–Hubbardton military road near Orwell, Vermont. The sign is located at the corner of Routes 22A and 73 West. *Courtesy of Lynne Venter*.

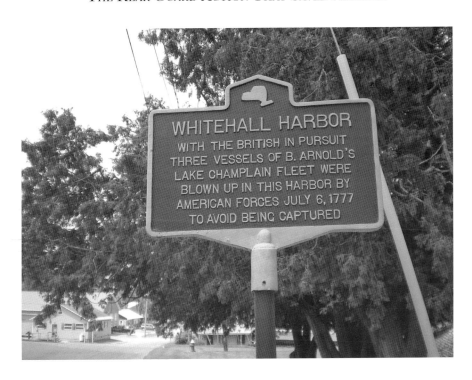

While General Burgoyne, aboard the *Royal George*, pursued Long's fleeing fleet of vessels and bateaux up the narrow stretch of Lake Champlain to Skenesborough, Brigadier Fraser organized his elite battalions for a march over the military road toward Hubbardton. Fraser's command would include ten companies of grenadiers under Major John Dyke Acland of the Twentieth Foot; ten companies of light infantry under Major Alexander Lindsay, the Earl of Balcarres, of the Fifty-third Foot; and two hat companies commanded by Major Robert Grant of the Twenty-fourth Foot, plus some Loyalists and Indians to serve as scouts. In all, Fraser took about 850 men from his Advance Corps. The military road's condition precluded Fraser from bringing along artillery with his column. The Scotsman's haste in chasing the rebels caused him to leave behind army surgeons, additional provisions, tents and extra ammunition. General Riedesel was ordered to follow Fraser with Breymann's Corps, his own Riedesel regiment and a Jäger company, adding another 1,100 to the column.[50]

No specific returns for the grenadier battalion or light infantry battalion exist to show the strength of each battalion. In General Burgoyne's return, dated July 1, 1777, the flank companies (i.e. the grenadier and light infantry companies) are grouped together with the battalion companies in their respective regiments. Regimental strengths are showed in aggregate, not as separate company returns added together. We know from Fraser's own report that he took a total of 850 troops with him to Hubbardton. It is unclear whether he was referring to the twenty-two different companies (ten grenadier, ten light infantry and two battalion or hat companies) or whether he included his scouts in this figure. A simple calculation would yield about 39 men per company without the scouts and 36 men per company, if the scouts were taken out of the 850 total. Admittedly, these are rough estimates, but they will be useful later in this study for analyzing how much space the several British units took up on the battlefield at Hubbardton.[51]

To block the redcoats' fast-moving pursuit, St. Clair selected Colonel Ebenezer Francis, an officer whom even Burgoyne acknowledged as "one of their best Officers." The colonel's regimental chaplain felt that "no officer [was] so noticed for his military accomplishments and regular life as he was. His conduct in the field is spoken of in the highest terms of praise." Francis's rear guard would consist of "chosen men" from his own Eleventh Massachusetts Continentals and picked units from other Patriot regiments. In all, he would command about 450 troops. As he moved behind St. Clair's main army, the thirty-four-year-old Medford native was ordered to gather "every living thing," meaning he was free to pick up stragglers and shirkers as well as any roaming herd animals that were found.[52]

A nineteenth-century pastoral view of the Hubbardton battlefield from Benson J. Lossing's *The Pictorial Field-Book of the Revolution* (1850).

It was a twenty-mile march southeast from Mount Independence to Hubbardton. The latter place was a small enclave of about nine hearty families who had been eking out a subsistence living in the Hampshire Grants wilderness for the last two years. Some of the hilly terrain had been cleared for farming, but most of the surrounding mountains remained forested. The John Selleck family had planted a cornfield a little northeast of their log cabin.[53]

About three miles northwest of Hubbardton, at Lacey's Camp, St. Clair was alerted that a party of Loyalists and Indians had already been through the tiny settlement. Lacey's Camp was a small clearing where a man named Lacey had built a log cabin that he had also used as a tavern.

According to one contemporary source, some village residents were attending church in a schoolhouse on Sunday morning when the services were loudly interrupted by the scouting party's blood-curdling war whoops and musket firing. Captain Alexander Fraser, Simon's nephew, commanded the Crown's men. He was ably assisted by a local Loyalist named Captain Justus

Sherwood, a twenty-five-year-old, well-educated officer who was tenacious in his support for King George. A skirmish erupted in which the local militia commander, Captain John Hall, was mortally wounded. Shot in the leg, Hall was further bayoneted by a Tory for good measure. Hall would die a month later. His two sons were later captured and taken to Fort Ticonderoga but made their escape. They avenged their father's death by fighting at Saratoga.[54]

This incident and other intelligence reported to St. Clair not only proved that lurking, ruthless marauders were skirting his army but also suggested that Fraser was in hot pursuit, looking for an already demoralized foe. Nevertheless, St. Clair was determined to move his army to Castleton and link up with Schuyler at Skenesborough, unaware that Long's fleet would soon be in shambles. St. Clair's soldiers would get a chance to rough up Captain Fraser's band later when he found them in Castleton. Undeterred, the Loyalists and Indians continued their mayhem, grabbing captives later in the day near Hubbardton.[55]

Swatting away a few King's men like Justus Sherwood was not St. Clair's only concern that night. Once he heard of Long's debacle at Skenesborough, St. Clair knew he'd have to take a wide, circuitous route through Rutland to rendezvous with the northern department's commander at Fort Edward.

About noontime on July 6, St. Clair's weary troops reached a narrow gap through Sargent Hill, which was locally called the "Saddle." Crews building the Mount Independence–Hubbardton military road in 1776 found the Saddle useful because this natural declivity avoided a higher climb over the top of Sargent Hill. From the Saddle, the military road descended about three-quarters of a mile to Sucker Brook, a small stream running through a narrow valley. Once across Sucker Brook, the military road skirted another elevation to the east—which would eventually be known as Monument Hill but had no geographic name in 1777. Running south near the base of Monument Hill, the military road then angled southeast between Monument Hill and a still unnamed hill to the south.

At this point, a soldier marching on the military road toward Castleton could look to his right, or southwest, and see an imposing elevation rising over 1,100 feet above the road. This cliff-like peak is sometimes called Zion Hill in older descriptions but is more popularly known as Mount Zion today.[56] Mount Zion has baffled some chroniclers of the action at Hubbardton because at least one contemporary account claims it was a factor in the battle. This misinterpretation sometimes confuses mapmakers who show British troops scaling Mount Zion in an effort to outflank the Americans. Anyone who visits the battlefield today will clearly see that Mount Zion

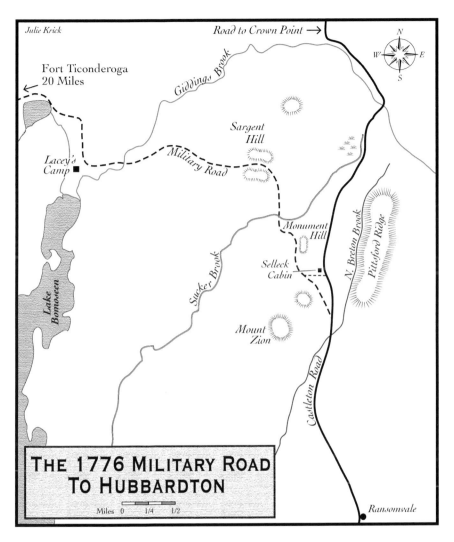

A map of the 1776 Mount Independence–Hubbardton military road. *Prepared by Julie Krick for the author.*

could not have been a factor in the fight because it is too high and too far for musket-toting troops to be within effective range. If anything, Mount Zion might have been used as a safe perch for Fraser's Indian and Loyalist scouts, a place where they could get a good view of the fighting.

Near the southwest slope of Monument Hill, the 1776 military road appears to split. A sharp turn left to the east would bring a soldier on a spur road that ended in front of the Selleck cabin. If the soldier did not take this spur, he would continue marching diagonally in a southeasterly direction until he met the Castleton Road. If he turned right, to the south, his march to Castleton would be about seven miles. If he turned left, to the north, he would pass the Selleck homestead and eventually connect with the old Crown Point military road, which was improved in 1772 to encourage settlement of the area.

The 1776 military road incorporated a section of the Castleton road until it reached Ransomvale, where it again turned diagonally to the southeast, eventually joining the old Crown Point military road, which ended in New Hampshire at the Fort at No. 4. Both the spur and a longer route to the Castleton road show up on Captain Johann H.D. Gerlach's 1777 map, drawn only days after the battle ended. Gerlach was a German staff officer who performed the duties of deputy quartermaster general under Riedesel. He was also a trained engineer who sketched a high-quality, detailed plan of the battlefield.[57]

Once the retreating column reached Hubbardton, St. Clair called a halt for about two hours. It was a blisteringly hot afternoon, so the rest was a relief

A section of the 1776 Mount Independence–Hubbardton military road near the Saddle of Sargent Hill. *Author's collection.*

for his sweating, grumbling and hungry soldiers. The army then continued on to Castleton, where it would camp for the night. Francis caught up with the column at Hubbardton, where Colonel Seth Warner took command of the rear guard with orders to follow the army. St. Clair also detached Colonel Nathan Hale (no relation to the Patriot spy of the same name who gave his life for his country) with his Second New Hampshire Continentals to support Warner and Francis. Hale had been trailing the main column because his regiment had been shepherding the column's sick, disabled and "feeble" who could not keep up with their regiments. Hale also had to keep them ahead of Francis's rear guard.[58]

St. Clair had chosen three Continental colonels with proven combat experience to protect his rear. With knowledge that Loyalists and Indians were lurking in the area, St. Clair wanted to redouble his effort to guard his rear. He wanted Warner to stay about two miles behind the army. Warner would have an estimated 900 fighting men available to prevent disaster, or up to 1,200, if stragglers and sick soldiers are counted. One analysis of the numbers engaged shows that Colonel Francis commanded 450 men as his rear guard contingent, Colonel Warner's Green Mountain Boys regiment mustered no more than 150 men, Colonel Hale's New Hampshire regiment counted about 235 soldiers and there might have been about 100 Vermont militiamen called up at Hubbardton. If an estimated 300 invalids, sick and intoxicated stragglers are counted, then Warner had approximately 1,235 men available to meet the pursuing British.[59]

Lying alongside North Breton Brook at Ransomvale about four miles south of Hubbardton were two Massachusetts militia regiments under Colonel Benjamin Bellows. These units were part of the main army, not Warner's command, but could be called on to go to Warner's assistance. One authority on Hubbardton believes, "It is possible that [St. Clair] wanted them between the strong rear guard and his main body as a measure for controlling them since [during] most of the march discipline problems had occurred in the militia regiments."[60]

The thirty-four-year-old Warner had an excellent reputation as a rear guard commander, earned during the northern army's retreat from Canada the previous year. A sympathetic biographer who knew Warner when the author was a youngster claimed his men had "unlimited confidence, in his judgment, his vigilance, his prudence and his unflinching courage" and "they loved him for his moral and social qualities." General Schuyler praised Warner to Washington for his service in the ill-fated Canadian campaign. During the American retreat from Canada, Warner was "always in the rear, picking up the wounded and

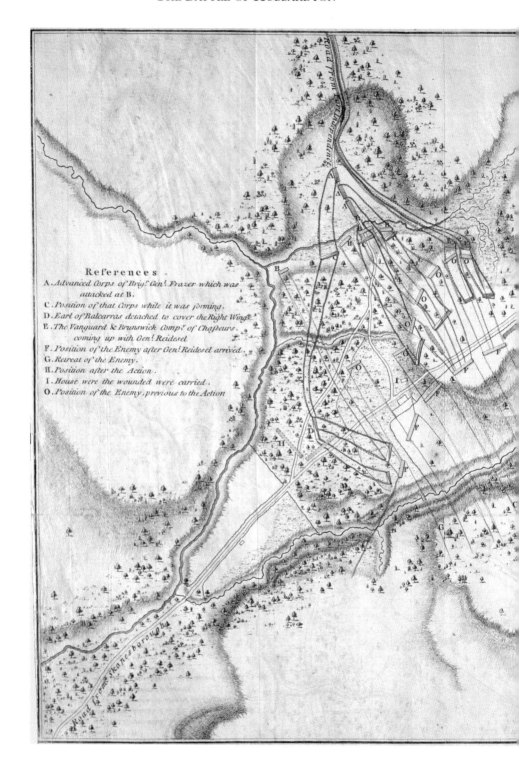

References

A . Advanced Corps of Brig.t Gen.l Frazer which was
    attacked at B.
C . Position of that Corps while it was forming.
D . Earl of Balcarras detached to cover the Right Wing.
E . The Vanguard & Brunswick Comp.y of Chaßeurs.
    coming up with Gen.l Reidesel
F . Position of the Enemy after Gen.l Reidesel arrived.
G . Retreat of the Enemy.
H . Position after the Action.
I . House were the wounded were carried.
O . Position of the Enemy, previous to the Action

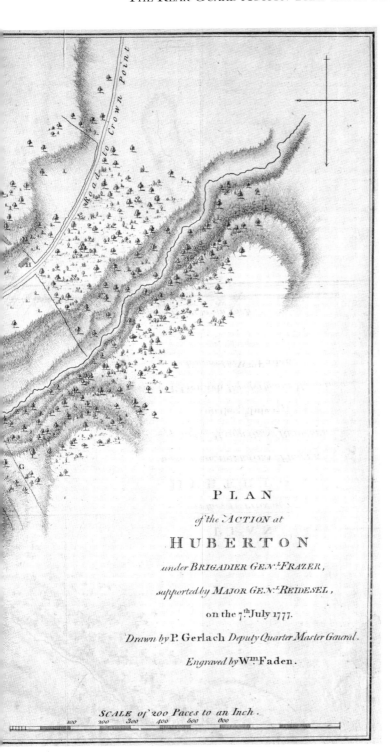

PLAN

of the ACTION *at*

HUBERTON

under BRIGADIER GE.N.^L FRAZER,

supported by MAJOR GE.N.^L REIDESEL,

on the 7th July 1777.

Drawn by P. Gerlach *Deputy Quarter Master General.*

Engraved by Wm Faden.

SCALE *of* 200 *Paces to an Inch.*

A copy of a map of the Hubbardton battlefield drawn by Captain Johann H.D. Gerlach, deputy quartermaster general and German engineer officer. Gerlach prepared this map within hours after the battle; it is the best and only representation of the battlefield with troop movements. This map appeared in General Burgoyne's *State of the Expedition from Canada*, in which he defended his actions during the campaign to Parliament. *Courtesy of the Hubbardton Battlefield Site and in author's collection.*

diseased, assisting and encouraging those who were least able to take care of themselves, and generally kept but a few miles in advance" of the enemy. Warner also was selected by the Dorset Convention to command the Green Mountain Boys regiment as lieutenant colonel over the archetypal Green Mountain Boy himself, Ethan Allen. No contemporary image exists of Warner, although he has been described as a "man of commanding appearance, more than six feet in height, with kindly though strongly chiseled features." It is said that Warner "was not given to advertising his achievements, preferring to let them speak for themselves." Words like "modest and unassuming," "useful," "cool and deliberate" and "energy, resolution and firmness" pepper his nineteenth-century biography, giving the impression that St. Clair made a wise choice when he selected Warner to command his rear guard at Hubbardton.[61]

An early twentieth-century military officer who wrote the standard work on Burgoyne's campaign, which stood for half a century, was less kind. Hoffman Nickerson opined that Seth Warner was "brave and patriotic, but a rough fellow, illiterate and undisciplined," who was responsible for a command failure at Hubbardton that resulted in a tactical defeat. Nickerson thought the American rear guard should have stayed closer to St. Clair's main army. But this criticism is really unwarranted due to the circumstances Warner faced on the late afternoon of July 6 and the early morning hours of July 7. Warner made the best of a bad situation, conducting himself in a manner that saved more of the northern army than was lost.[62]

Colonel Francis joined Warner and Hale at Hubbardton at about 4:00 p.m. He had outdistanced the pursuing British under Fraser, but not by much. A young fifer in Hale's Second New Hampshire Regiment named Ebenezer Fletcher had fallen behind, having recently had a bout of measles, and was not "able to march with the main body." Swept up by Francis's command, Fletcher later recorded his experience as part of the rear guard: "By sunrise the enemy had landed from their boats, and pursued us so closely as to fire on our rear. A large body of the enemy followed us all day, but kept so far behind as not to be wholly discovered."[63]

Once Francis arrived, Warner called a meeting of the three officers in the Selleck cabin. It was at this council of war that Warner made the decision not to move his command but wait a day until the men were rested and had some food in their bellies. It had been a grueling twenty-mile march in the last twelve hours over a rugged road. He probably did not have much of a choice. If he moved as St. Clair expected, undoubtedly he would have left hundreds of soldiers behind, most likely to fall into the enemy's hands. His experience during the retreat from Canada the previous year perhaps reminded him of the challenges he faced now

A statue of Colonel Seth Warner at the Bennington Battle Monument. There are no contemporary images of Warner. *Courtesy of Michael P. Gabriel.*

at Hubbardton. In Warner, St. Clair had picked the right man for a difficult job. The Vermonter was also aware that two unruly militia regiments were blocking the road at Ransomvale. Plus Warner had a good defensive position—or at least that's what he thought—on Monument Hill.[64]

St. Clair would later state that he was surprised that Warner disobeyed orders. He was also unforgiving of the colonel's actions in his court-martial

Remains of the cellar of the John Selleck cabin at the corner of the Castleton road and the military road spur. The Selleck cabin served as Seth Warner's temporary headquarters before the battle and as a hospital for the wounded after the action. *Author's collection.*

testimony. St. Clair obtusely reasoned that Warner's decision prevented him from reaching Skenesborough in time to save the stores entrusted to Long. St. Clair's questionable logic also claimed that not only could he have prevented the catastrophe at Skenesborough, but he probably could have "cut off that party of the enemy which pursued them."[65] St. Clair's judgment was likely influenced by the pressure of his court-martial because it's difficult to see how his worn-out Continentals would have done any better against Burgoyne's regulars than Warner did against Fraser and Riedesel. On the other hand, Warner's decision might have saved the northern army from a major defeat and allowed St. Clair to rally on Schuyler at Fort Edward.

Warner's decision to stay put might also have been based on the confidence he had in his two subordinates. Like Warner, Ebenezer Francis was thirty-four years old and had been in the army since the siege of Boston. He started the war as a militia captain but quickly rose to colonel in the Continental line. He would prove himself a stubborn fighter in the upcoming engagement with Fraser's regulars. One military historian has concluded that Francis's Eleventh Massachusetts was "perhaps the best disciplined of all the Continentals in St.

Clair's force." Colonel Nathan Hale, also thirty-four, had been active in local politics before the war in his native New Hampshire. When hostilities broke out on April 19, 1775, at Lexington and Concord, Captain Hale formed up his company of minutemen and marched to Cambridge, Massachusetts, where he joined the fledgling Patriot army surrounding Boston. Shortly afterward, he would be promoted to major in the Third New Hampshire. He was at Bunker Hill. He was advanced to lieutenant colonel and then colonel of the Second New Hampshire Regiment Continental Line. Hale served under Washington in the 1776 battles around New York City and in New Jersey before his regiment was transferred to the northern department in 1777. Hale had combat experience but a questionable record. His character and behavior at Trenton were reviewed in a formal inquiry. The charges were subsequently dismissed, but a dark cloud followed Hale to Hubbardton.

Warner selected Hale for the difficult assignment of protecting the sick, disabled men and stragglers camped in the valley below Monument Hill. Unfortunately, Hale would not measure up to his commander's expectations.

On the morning of July 7, therefore, Warner had two battle-tested, if not perfect, subordinates to lean on, now that he decided to stay an extra night at Hubbardton.[66]

The first precaution Warner took as rear guard commander was to protect the sick and disabled stragglers lounging in the low country west of Monument Hill near Sucker Brook. Warner ordered a hastily constructed log breastwork thrown up on the south side of the stream. This was probably a makeshift barrier, not meant to be a formal earthwork. Captain James Carr's company from Hale's Second New Hampshire remained in the valley near Sucker Brook guarding the stragglers and acting as a first line of defense if the British attacked down the military road. Warner also established a lookout post on the west side of Sargent Hill where the military road ascended the Saddle. These pickets would provide an early warning alert if they spotted redcoats in the distance.

One chronicler of the 1777 campaign faults Warner and his subordinates for not "sending a patrol back down the road to see if they were being pursued." This comment is an unfair armchair general's assessment formed from hindsight. Warner only needed to know if the British were coming, and a few pickets could do that job as well as an organized patrol of several dozen or one hundred men. This same critic feels that "Warner probably was overconfident" at Hubbardton. No evidence exists to prove this was the case. In fact, it was not in Warner's character to exude such a trait. He inspired confidence in his men, but he was not one to boast or brag. Warner was making the best of a bad

A modern-day view of the Sargent Hill "Saddle" from the bottomland near Sucker Brook. The Fuller family barn is on the left. *Author's collection.*

situation as he dealt with part of a demoralized, retreating army that needed some rest to fight another day. Moreover, Warner did send a two-hundred-man reconnaissance force north toward the old Crown Point road in search of the Loyalist and Indian party St. Clair had heard about earlier in the day. He knew area inhabitants had been attacked, so this patrol was sent to assist them as well. This scouting operation came up empty-handed. It was supposed to return to Warner's camp by 7:00 a.m.[67]

Warner had his regiments bivouac on the east side of Monument Hill on a descending plateau that extended on both sides of the Castleton road. His water source was North Breton Brook. On the east side of the road was a high log fence built to protect farmer Selleck's cornfield. The high ground to his west, later known as Monument Hill, appeared ideal for defensive tactics. With these prudent actions completed by nightfall on July 6, Warner believed he was secure until morning, when he would commence his march to Castleton and rejoin St. Clair.[68]

A factor that might have influenced Warner's decision to stay put were the two militia regiments straddling the Castleton road about three miles south at

Ransomvale. Did Warner consider these troops the rear of St. Clair's army? If he did, then he was following his commander's orders. The record is silent as to what Warner's thoughts were on these units. Two commentators on the battle give Warner the benefit of the doubt. Because the two militia regiments were just within the Castleton town line, John Williams has concluded that "Warner possibly felt that he was in compliance with the orders and doctrine of rear guard employment in maintaining a reasonable distance from the main body." Williams, of course, had the benefit of hindsight and the ability to measure where the town line falls. It is doubtful that Warner knew the unreliable militia regiments provided him with a defense based on boundary lines. John P. Clements, who studied the battle for years, opines that until the troops at Ransomvale moved forward, Warner felt he could not move his own command down the road. As Clement reasons, "Under the circumstances, it is logical to conclude that Warner acted as a rear guard commander should act."[69]

It is more likely that Warner's concern for the condition of the sick, disabled and stragglers, scattered below the crest of Monument Hill in the low area around Sucker Brook, was the main factor that caused him to remain another night at Hubbardton. The position occupied by Bellows's command at Ransomvale was irrelevant. It appears that Warner was forced by circumstances beyond his control to make the decision he did to stay put. It was a logical choice because of his experience during the retreat from Canada. Warner's character probably influenced his decision to linger at Hubbardton more than any other factor. It was fortunate for St. Clair that he did.

Back at Mount Independence, Simon Fraser managed to get his plundering regulars under control and ready to march. It was 5:00 a.m. when he started east on the Hubbardton road. Fraser took the normal military precaution of sending out scouts to avoid surprise. He knew the Americans were ahead of him—about four miles by Fraser's estimate—and he wanted to catch up with them as soon as possible. Fraser's 850-man column had Grant's two hat companies of the Twenty-fourth Foot in the lead, followed by Lindsay's light infantry battalion, with Acland's grenadier battalion bringing up the rear. Why Lindsay's more agile troops did not lead the column is unrecorded.[70]

The redcoats marched nine miles before coming to a creek where the men had time to quench their thirst. At this point, not only did the British find water but also two fat "Bullocks" roaming the trail. They secured the cattle for a hearty roast beef meal later in the day. Fraser's troops ran into a contingent of twenty rebels near the watering hole who were "all very much in liquor." Fraser took a few minutes to scribble a message to Burgoyne, which Captain

Campbell of the Twenty-ninth Foot delivered for his commander. Fraser told Burgoyne he smelled more rebels not far ahead and he meant to attack them—a trait his commander appreciated in his aggressive subordinate.

The brigadier also requested Burgoyne to send him the remainder of the Advance Corps in support or any other "*British if possible*" (emphasis in the original). To Fraser's chagrin, Burgoyne opted to send troops under Riedesel. Sending the German general would mean that Fraser would be outranked if the Scotsman came close enough to engage the enemy and both officers were on the field simultaneously. This was not an appealing situation for Fraser, who wanted to handle the situation on his own.[71]

Now refreshed, Fraser moved his column another four miles before halting again. He had the two steers roasted by the side of another creek, which hardly satisfied his famished soldiers. As one grenadier officer told his journal, "without bread," the young bulls were "next to nothing among so many" men for the next two days.[72]

While his men were eating, Fraser was interrogating a rebel who had potentially useful information. The straggler confirmed that Colonel Francis commanded the Patriot rear guard. The derelict was not as knowledgeable about Francis's commitment to the cause of independence as he pretended. Sitting in front of the redcoat brigadier, the prisoner brazenly claimed that Francis would freely give himself up as a prisoner, if only Fraser would guarantee his safety from the feared "savages." According to this miscreant, Burgoyne's earlier threat to give "stretch" to his Indian allies, if the rebels did not abandon their cause, had put fear in Francis's heart and perhaps a few other colonists. Obviously, such a lame attempt to save this deserter's skin did not reflect the true grit of the brave Francis. Fraser tried to reach Francis by using his captive as bait, but the colonel "paid no other attention to [Fraser's] message." The brigadier, however, was convinced Francis quickened his pace as a result of his entreaty.[73]

About four o'clock in the afternoon, the same time that Francis's rear guard was stepping into Hubbardton, Fraser was surprised to find troops coming up on his rear. They were not the redcoats he had so earnestly requested but a contingent of "Chasseurs" or Jäger. The Jäger were special fighting units developed by Frederick the Great to act as light infantry. Their name literally meant "games-keeper" or "huntsman" because they were recruited from the German forests. Jäger were known as excellent marksmen. Like British light infantry companies, the Jäger were usually attached to line regiments as a separate company. They donned green uniforms to indicate their special status. Jäger carried short-barrel rifles that were accurate and easy to load and carry. The Jäger were used as scouts, skirmishers and sharpshooters. "Although it happened but rarely, [the

Major General Baron Friedrich Adolphus von Riedesel (1738–1800). *Courtesy of the National Archives, 111-SC-92607.*

Jäger] could also fight in line like a musketeer," according to one study. While Fraser was disappointed to see the Jäger arrive in his rear on July 6, he was probably silently thrilled with their service the next day.[74]

Riding up an hour after the Jäger appeared was General Riedesel, who informed Fraser that his Germans would support the British advance and then march to Skenesborough to rejoin the main army. Riedesel told Fraser he had about 1,100 troops under his command. In the advance guard was the Jäger company and about 80 grenadiers from Breymann's Corps, in all about 180 men. Unfortunately, in his equally hasty departure, Riedesel failed to bring any extra food, ammunition, surgeons or medical supplies. More troubling for Fraser, however, was that the remainder of his own Advance Corps had not been ordered to follow him. Fraser's bruised ego was quite evident later in a private letter he wrote to his friend John Robinson when he candidly acknowledged that he "felt much hurt to be embarrassed with a senior." Fraser took it as a slight that his friend Burgoyne had sent a major general to his aid. Fraser probably read more into Burgoyne's decision than the reality of the situation. Fraser later claimed there "were persons jealous of all my poor endeavors" who were trying to thwart his good service to the Crown. However, there is no evidence to support Fraser's paranoia or that Burgoyne had sinister designs when it came to army politics. Burgoyne liked Fraser and enjoyed having him under his command. Burgoyne sent Riedesel because his German troops were on the east side of Mount Independence close to the Hubbardton road.[75] Fraser was within hours of engaging the enemy in combat. He should have been more concerned about the lack of an ammunition reserve, no extra provisions and no surgeons than his own personal conceit.

Nevertheless, if battlefield decisions were to be made, Fraser worried that he would have to defer to Riedesel, his junior in age but not rank. This perceived snub, although without validity, undoubtedly affected the way

Fraser brought on the engagement with Warner at Hubbardton. It could have cost Fraser the battle had Riedesel's Germans not saved the day.

During the meeting between Fraser and Riedesel, it was agreed that the brigadier would march another three miles or until he found a water source and bivouac for the night. Riedesel's Germans would move up and take the former British resting spot that evening for their camp. Both Fraser and Riedesel would start forward early the next morning from their respective locations. Still trying to maintain some form of independent command, Fraser reiterated to the German nobleman that he had "discretionary powers to attack the Enemy where-ever I could come up on them, & I determined to do it." Writing later in his memoirs in the third person, much like the great commander Julius Caesar, the German general would state that "in case General Fraser found the enemy too strong for him he was to wait for General Riedesel and thus offer a united front to the enemy." Fraser said he would break camp at 3:00 a.m. the next day. Riedesel, not one to cause dissention, agreed to Fraser's plan; he would move out early as well.[76]

On July 7, at the appointed time, both contingents of Burgoyne's army near Hubbardton moved out. Fraser's column seems to have moved at a quicker pace than its German counterpart. Perhaps it was Fraser's personality that influenced his marching speed. The German regulars did not maintain the same pace. Although there was only a three-mile difference between their camps the night before, during the hike toward Sargent Hill, the heavily equipped Brunswickers fell behind. Riedesel's wise decision to put his agile Jäger out in front along with some elite grenadiers would prove beneficial later in the day.

After marching about a mile from his bivouac the previous night, Fraser came to a clearing in the woods alongside the military road. Here he detached an officer—perhaps it was a Captain Mackey—to await in darkness the oncoming Germans. Fraser smelled trouble up ahead, and he wanted to make sure the German general was urged on if firing was heard down the road. Fraser's precaution in leaving a redcoat officer seems a bit like having a witness for the defense if things went awry that day.[77]

The British marched another two miles. Sunlight had barely burned off the dusk of early morning. An advance guard of vigilant Loyalists and Indians were making their way along both sides of the military road. Suddenly, musket shots and cries rang out from the silent forest. The sounds came from the head of Fraser's column where the scouts were intent on finding the enemy. As the scouts were carefully picking their way through the

The ambush site on the Mount Independence–Hubbardton military road where American pickets fired on the lead elements of Fraser's column before retreating back to defensive lines along Sucker Brook, as pointed out to the author by Carl Fuller. *Author's collection.*

Saddle of Sargent Hill, American pickets fired on them from a rocky height above the military road. After a few shots, the rebels disappeared, falling back about a half mile toward Warner's encampment near Sucker Brook. It was probably around 5:00 a.m. These unfriendly missiles were the first shots of the battle of Hubbardton.[78]

4

FIRST BLOOD AT SUCKER BROOK

Fraser immediately alerted Major Grant, who commanded two companies of the Twenty-fourth Foot in the van, to prepare his men for an attack. The light infantry battalion under Major Lindsay, the Earl of Balcarres, would come in on Grant's left with Major Acland's grenadier battalion to act as a reserve. Next, Fraser ordered the officer commanding his Loyalist and Indian scouts to reconnoiter the American camp of sick and disabled stragglers near Sucker Brook and guarded by Captain Carr's company of Hale's Second New Hampshire Continentals. As the British entered the down-slope portion of the Saddle, they would find high ground on both sides of the military road—a great opportunity for an ambush. The forested ground was rugged; the road scattered with tree stumps made the going tough. (It remains so even today.) One commentator on the battle believes that "logically, the reconnaissance would have taken place to the west of the American camp, well out on the flanks to avoid detection."[79]

One result of this scouting effort gave Fraser information that surprised him. The enemy near Hubbardton was in much larger numbers than he had anticipated. In all likelihood, the Scotsman thought he was dealing with Francis's rear guard, a unit about regimental strength. That turned out not to be the case.

The Indian and Loyalist band may have gone as much as a mile around the Patriots' position to assess the enemy's depth. Sneaking around the American perimeter, some Indians quickly dispatched a rebel picket with the tomahawk. They were gone about an hour. Some scouts might have climbed Mount Zion, the dominant eminence in the area, to get a bird's-eye view of the situation.

What they saw must have amazed them. Instead of a paltry rear guard of a few hundred men that could be easily swept aside by seasoned regulars, the redcoats were facing a Continental force that actually outnumbered Fraser's command. Whether the scouting party was at the summit's escarpment or only a few hundred feet up the mountain, they could easily see three American regiments forming up on the Castleton road. Some chroniclers of the battle think at this point "it is also probable that Tory spies within the American bivouac were in liaison with their counterparts in the British scouting party and might have rendezvoused with them." It is true that Fraser later said he "was then in the most disaffected part of America, every person a Spy."[80] Regardless how he got his intelligence, the Scotsman now knew he was in for a fight.

Meanwhile, back at the Selleck cabin, Warner's temporary command post near the Castleton road, the Vermont colonel was meeting with Francis and Hale. His men had been up at sunrise, building fires, fixing breakfast and packing up their belongings in preparation for their march to link up with St. Clair's main army. The plan was to stay behind the Patriot army as it made its way to Skenesborough to join with Colonel Long's contingent and then march south through Fort Ann to Fort Edward on the Hudson River. Warner knew shots had been fired and that the British were coming. He probably had no idea of the enemy's strength. At the same time, a mounted courier rode up to the cabin with a message from the army's commander. Plans had changed. St. Clair's other division had experienced a catastrophe at Skenesborough. Burgoyne's sailors had managed to break the log and chain boom across Lake Champlain, allowing the British army and some Germans to follow on Long's heels. The result was a disaster for Long and his command.

St. Clair's route was now compromised. He would have to change direction and head east before moving south to join Schuyler. Warner's instructions were to do the same. Instead of finding the army at Castleton, the Green Mountain officer was to march his men to Rutland, southeast of his initial target. Warner's intention was to move as soon as the errant two-hundred-man patrol he had sent out earlier looking for the Loyalist and Indian raiders returned. His patrol was scheduled to be back at camp by 7:00 a.m. Warner also had to be concerned whether the two willful militia regiments under Bellows at Ransomvale had moved forward.

Warner ordered his own Green Mountain regiment of six companies to form up on the Castleton road south of the Selleck cabin. This column stretched about three hundred yards from the intersection of the spur of the military road down the Castleton road. Behind the Vermonters, lining up north of the cabin for another three hundred yards were the mixed companies of Francis's

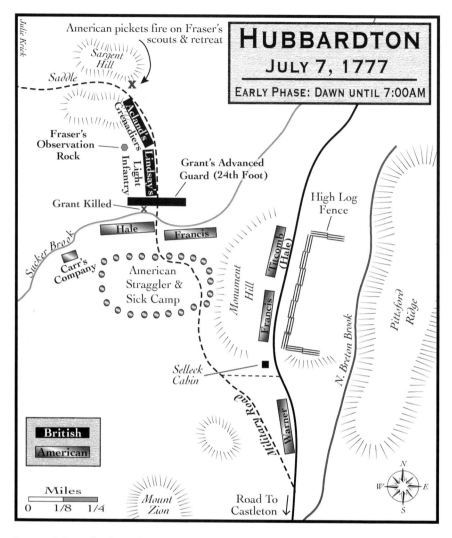

A map of the early phase: dawn until 7:00 a.m. *Prepared by Julie Krick for the author.*

rear guard, which included parts of his own Eleventh Massachusetts as well as companies from Colonel Joseph Cilley's First New Hampshire and Colonel Alexander Scammell's Third New Hampshire Regiments—units selected for their reliability. Following his return from the meeting at the Selleck cabin, Francis ordered Captain Moses Greenleaf to "march the regiment with the greatest expedition, or the enemy will be upon us." Greenleaf scribbled in his diary that it was 7:15 a.m. when he got Francis's order. Francis's urgency indicates that it was Warner's intention not to bring on a general engagement at Hubbardton if it could be avoided. His men had received a night's rest. They should be ready to continue the general retreat to Castleton and beyond.[81]

Behind the end of Francis's agglomerated unit was part of Hale's Second New Hampshire, stretching about 250 yards under the temporary command of Major Benjamin Titcomb. The regiment had eight companies altogether, but the unit was divided by its current deployment. Titcomb was in charge of the New Hampshire companies on the Castleton road because the regimental commander, Colonel Hale, had moved to the bottom land below Monument Hill to be with Captain Carr and some other troops who were guarding the encampment near Sucker Brook.[82]

Monday, July 7, would challenge Warner's leadership skills, his grit and his determination to take on the King's army. His frontier upbringing and previous military experiences would serve him well as he prepared for a fight with Brigadier Fraser.

Early on the morning of July 7, sixteen-year-old Joseph Bird was casually adding chocolate to the water he was boiling for his liquid breakfast. Chocolate was a common ingredient for soldiers serving in St. Clair's northern army who wanted to jumpstart their day with a jolt of caffeine. The young soldier's campfire was in the valley below Monument Hill near Sucker Brook. He and his comrades had slept the chilly night before on the ground in a clearing wrapped in their blankets. Even in July, there is a coolness that arrives after sunset in Vermont's mountainous countryside. Bird was preparing to leave Hubbardton like all the other men in Warner's command. Bird had served at Fort Ticonderoga the previous February, first as a surgeon's assistant in the Sixth Massachusetts and now in Captain John Chadwick's company, a unit in Colonel Samuel Brewer's Twelfth Massachusetts Continental regiment. In later oral testimony, the Connecticut native doesn't say why he was near the stream, whether he was a straggler, disabled or aiding the sick who had gathered below the hill. His campsite, however, put him at the very crucible of first light's action.

Bird was walking down the military road near Monument Hill, heading south, carrying his cup of hot chocolate, when one of his comrades in the Twelfth Massachusetts "jumped up and cocked his gun to fire." An officer shouted to the soldier to hold his fire. Bird turned around to see what alarmed the man. To his amazement, Bird witnessed "the enemy aforming [sic] about 15 rods from us."[83] Apparently, Simon Fraser had waited long enough for Riedesel to bring up his Germans.

Fraser had assessed the intelligence reports brought in by his Loyalist and Indian scouts. The Americans appeared to be in significant numbers in the

Sucker Brook valley and along the Castleton road. One British officer claimed in his journal that the number was "about 2000 Rebels" near Hubbardton. Another officer agreed.[84] But the veteran brigadier was not to be deterred. He was working against the clock. If Warner marched before the British were able to launch an attack, the rebels would likely get away. Waiting for Riedesel and his Brunswickers to come up would add depth to his attack, but it might also upstage his command decisions, as the German major general would outrank him.

Fraser had served under Major General James Wolfe at Quebec in 1759 during the French and Indian War. Perhaps he reflected on the chances Wolfe took by sending his troops up the cliffs and narrow path above L'Anse-au-Foulon in the inky darkness of September 12, almost eighteen years earlier. It was a chancy gamble that paid off, contributing significantly to Great Britain's conquest of Canada. Now, perhaps Fraser saw that it was his turn, like Wolfe, to throw the dice in a bid to crush the Patriot rear guard and destroy what was left of St. Clair's army. Burgoyne himself was famously known as an old gamester, a frequent card player at London's best private clubs. Fraser would imitate his commander today, not at a gaming table where money is won or lost, but on the field of battle where brave men's lives would be at stake.

By about 7:00 a.m., Fraser had made his decision to attack. He had sent enough messages urging Riedesel to hurry. One early study of the battle has Fraser opposing an attack until his German support arrives, but Major Robert Grant "glows with ardors to begin the attack, and Fraser at length consents." Whether this fanciful pleading from Grant had any effect on Fraser or whether it even happened is mere speculation. It is one of those apocryphal incidents that gets repeated in various accounts without a substantive original source to back it up. A similar local tradition has Fraser climbing on a high rock on the south side of Sargent Hill to get a better look at what he was facing in the valley below the hill. In fact, Fraser makes no mention of climbing on a rock to view the terrain. There is, however, a rock near the military road that would meet the description of a good lookout post for the brigadier. And finally, a nineteenth-century artist and chronicler of Revolutionary War battlefields and historic sites, who tapped local lore for most of his narratives, contends there is a boulder near the battlefield, called Sentinel Rock, that the first British soldier down the military road stood on to see the American encampment

Opposite, top: Sucker Brook near Monument Hill, where the surrounding ground is swampy due to modern-day beaver dams, per Carl Fuller. *Author's collection.*

Opposite, bottom: Trace of the 1776 Mount Independence–Hubbardton military road on the east side of Sargent Hill. *Author's collection.*

below Monument Hill. The redcoat was shot by a rebel picket before he could jump off the rock. This account is challenged by a map made shortly after the battle by a German officer, which puts the battleground beyond the rock.[85]

Nevertheless, Fraser ordered Grant forward with his two leading companies of the Twenty-fourth Foot, approximately seventy-five men. Grant was considered a "very gallant and brave officer." The brigadier planned to open the battle with Grant and Lindsay's light infantry battalion, with Acland's grenadiers serving as a reserve. Grant advanced down the military road toward Sucker Brook until he had enough room to spread his companies into battle formation. He would have encountered some wetlands near the stream that still exist today. The Americans would respond by forming a scattered defense south of Sucker Brook.[86]

The young fifer Ebenezer Fletcher was following orders that morning to "refresh and be ready for marching." He was expecting it to be a normal day of marching, if that was possible in these turbulent days following the evacuation of Mount Independence. Among his comrades, Fletcher observed, "some were eating, some were cooking, and all in a very unfit posture for battle." It wasn't long after sunlight appeared in the bottomland valley that the regimental musician heard one of his fellow soldiers cry, "The enemy are upon us!" To Fletcher's surprise, he looked up from his breakfast to see a formation of red-coated British infantry in line of battle.

At that point, Fletcher said, "orders came to lay down our packs and be ready for action." The redcoats unleashed a volley that unnerved the Americans, including Fletcher, and caused some of the rebels to scamper into nearby woods. A confident Captain James Carr ran to the front, reassuring his New Hampshire boys with inspiring words as he said, "My lads advance, we shall best them yet." A few of the men rallied behind Carr, including young Ebenezer. As the firing intensified, "every man was trying to secure himself behind girdled trees, which were standing on the place of action." Fletcher found his own protection behind a tree and fired his musket. He reloaded, but this time his gun misfired. Undeterred, the young rebel again loaded his piece and brought it to his shoulder, but before he could discharge his shot, Ebenezer felt a sharp pain in the small of his back. A musket ball—whether from a Brown Bess or friendly fire, it mattered little—hit a mark; Fletcher fell down with his gun still cocked.

The stunned young man looked around for help. Fletcher spied his uncle, Daniel Foster, standing not far away, so he crawled over to reveal his wound. Uncle Daniel and another soldier quickly carried Fletcher back to the shelter of a large tree, which he shared with another man who was wailing in pain.

By now, British grenadiers were bearing down on the faltering American line; it was every man for himself as Fletcher saw it. He decided concealment was his best option.

For a time, Fletcher hid himself under a fallen timber; some of Acland's grenadiers were so close to the log, the young fifer could have touched them, but he remained in his hiding place until the firing stopped. After the battle, Fletcher was discovered by redcoats mopping up the area. He was brought to a makeshift field hospital to dress his wound. By this time, British surgeons had arrived at Hubbardton. Two doctors assured the young fifer that he would most likely recover from his wound.[87]

It is likely that elements of Hale's New Hampshire regiment came down off Monument Hill or were already in the valley with Hale to join Carr's company and the mixed group of stragglers and disabled. Some of Francis's men, too, might have joined the fight in the low area before retreating back to the top of Monument Hill. It is difficult to estimate how many Patriots were in the bottomland opposing the redcoats, but it must have been several hundred. The Americans might have thrown up some impediments near the stream like a crude abatis of sharpened tree limbs to protect their vulnerable encampment. The rebels' resistance was somewhat successful because it forced Fraser to deploy Grant's companies and Lindsay's infantry battalion in the low area below Monument Hill, a classic delaying strategy in eighteenth-century warfare due to the amount of time it took to maneuver companies and battalions. However, the British were only slowed down, not stopped, by the American actions south of Sucker Brook.[88]

The Second New Hampshire men and those sick and disabled who were able, as Fletcher recounts, retreated into the woods but kept firing from behind trees, stumps and fallen timber as the British pursued them. Some of them might have joined Warner's line near the Castleton road, but most probably fled the scene. Most of the wounded and stragglers were gobbled up by Acland as his grenadiers overran the American encampment south of Sucker Brook.[89]

Over on the downward slope of Sargent Hill, Fraser decided to personally lead Lindsay's light infantry battalion, perhaps because this was the Earl of Balcarres's first combat. At first, the light infantry marched directly behind Grant. Then, Fraser moved to Grant's left. Grant engaged the rebels at Sucker Brook, where the two battalion companies began to take heavy casualties, which included Grant. The major was shot dead before he was able to cross the stream. Twenty-one other redcoats also fell near their commander. The only description of Grant's death comes from a well-used and graphic contemporary account by a British volunteer officer whose veracity has been challenged by some historians. As Lieutenant Thomas Anburey told it in his reminiscences: "Upon his coming up with the enemy, [Grant] got upon the stump of a tree to reconnoiter, and had hardly given the men orders to fire when he was struck by a rifle ball, fell off of the tree, and never uttered another syllable." Most historians of the campaign agree that Anburey was at Hubbardton, but he sometimes contrived his facts to make a good story. Unquestionably, the story of Grant's death is an exciting depiction. However, there were no riflemen in Warner's command; they only carried smoothbore muskets. Only the German Jäger carried rifles at Hubbardton. Most likely, Grant was killed when the Twenty-fourth Foot sustained heavy casualties from an American volley unleashed on Grant's troops as they approached Sucker Brook.[90]

FRASER ATTACKS MONUMENT HILL

With the remnants of Grant's platoons trading shots with the enemy, Fraser's attention was drawn to "a pretty steep hill" on his left. Marching at the head of Lindsay's ten light infantry companies, Fraser suddenly called a halt. It was probably near 7:30 a.m. He faced the light infantry companies to the left in a battalion front, approximately 375 men. Once the scarlet-coated battalion was formed, the gallant Scotsman "ran up the hill" with his men, drums beating and soldiers yelling. Sensing danger, Colonel Francis ordered the companies standing in column on the Castleton road to face right and meet the oncoming redcoats. Like two freight trains crashing head on in the early morning light, Fraser met Francis's men halfway up Monument Hill. A grenadier officer, who was watching the attack before being called from his reserve position, recorded in his journal that no matter what obstructions the Americans had placed on Monument Hill, they had "no effect on the ardor always shewn [*sic*] by British Troops, who with the greatest steadiness and resolution, mounted the hill amidst showers of balls mixed with buck shot, which they plentifully bestowed amongst us."[91]

Some of the rebels' buck and ball found their marks. As the light infantry hit the Americans on Monument Hill, Lieutenant James Haggart received a ball in each eye, killing him instantly. Haggart was a marine officer with just two years of service on his record who must have accompanied Fraser as a volunteer, knowing there would be action to see under the Scotsman.

A twentieth-century depiction of Colonel Ebenezer Francis's troops defending Monument Hill early in the battle by Roy H. Heinrich (1938). *Courtesy of the National Life Group, Montpelier, Vermont.*

Lieutenant James Douglas of the Twenty-ninth Foot was also killed early in the fight. Another young officer, Douglas, had been wounded in the assault on the hill. As he was being carried off the field, another ball slammed into his chest without missing his heart. These two early casualties would be followed by many more as the British fought Warner's men in close combat that day.[92]

The battle was now for the possession of Monument Hill. Fraser's report indicates that he charged up the hill with his light infantry and "we met the Rebels endeavouring [*sic*] to get possession" of it. This statement would indicate that Warner did not have any men posted at the military crest of the hill—that is, a few dozen feet below the actual crest—to meet the attacking redcoats. He might not have had any troops on the actual crest of Monument Hill either. No senior American officer wrote an after-action report of the battle. A literal reading of Fraser's report gives the impression that the Patriots had to meet the British on the run, rather than being stationed in a strong defensive position.

An American captain's diary entry indicates that the Patriots were not guarding Monument Hill, albeit it being an excellent defensive position. Moses Greenleaf claimed in his daybook that "at twenty minutes past 7, the enemy appeared within gun-shot of us; we fac'd to the right, when the firing began, which lasted until ¾ past Eight a.m. without Cessation."[93] The captain's words suggest that his unit was on the Castleton road waiting to march, rather than in line of battle ready to meet the enemy. The Americans had to turn right to meet Fraser's infantrymen. If the British were within "gun-shot" of the Americans, it would mean they were within eighty to two hundred yards of the enemy. This tempting bit of information leads to the assumption that Fraser gained Monument Hill without much opposition, only to face a horrendous fire once his men crested the top of the hill. The counterattack by Francis stalled the British light infantrymen and probably raised Fraser's concern for the whereabouts of Riedesel.

Today, anyone visiting the Hubbardton battlefield can easily see that Monument Hill offers an ideal defensive position. Why Warner did not take advantage of this terrain seems, at first, a mystery. Had his men dug in at the military crest of Monument Hill, he might have repulsed a significant portion of Fraser's force and perhaps won a stunning victory. Certainly his Continentals would have inflicted serious casualties on the British as Fraser's men had the disadvantage of advancing up the slope and receiving fire from above them. As it was, the battle was a bloody slugfest for the redcoats. But with an advantageous position like Monument Hill, it seems like Warner's men could have inflicted even more fatalities. Instead, the Americans had to attack the British at the same time as they were being attacked—not an enviable situation. Fraser's red-coated regulars were seasoned veterans from previous campaigns, some having seen "first blood" action as far back as at Lexington and Concord in 1775.

So why did the Americans have to come on the run to reach the crest of Monument Hill? The answer may lie in Warner's original intentions on July 7. By 7:00 a.m. or so, he knew the British were coming. Shots had been fired almost two hours earlier by his pickets in the Saddle of Sargent Hill. He also knew from St. Clair's frantic message that things had gone terribly wrong at Skenesborough. Moreover, he had to deal with several hundred sick and disabled men, plus the likes of recalcitrant stragglers. Warner had a lot on his plate. His orders that morning to his subordinate commanders were to get their regiments up and in column of march before the British caught up with them. At 7:00 a.m., it seems that Warner was thinking only of flight and really had no intention of taking on Fraser's troops in a pitched battle.

In addition, Warner had no intelligence telling him how large the pursuing force was. Warner could be faulted for this shortcoming. But his mission was not to bring on a full-scale engagement, where having a good idea of his opponent's strength would be essential. His goal was to keep his regiments moving. He probably would have marched sooner if his soldiers were physically capable of continuing their retreat. It was not just the stragglers and the disabled who were a problem. Many of his Continentals, no doubt, were plain worn out from their blistery, hot march the previous day. If Warner meant to fight at Hubbardton, he most likely would have provided for a defense of Monument Hill and, likewise, protected his vulnerable left flank to the south. He did not take these precautions because his goal was to keep moving. As a rear guard commander, Warner's job was to delay the enemy, not bring on a full-scale engagement, if at all possible. Warner, however, was unable to avoid this situation. It could have been a more costly mistake had not it been for the grit and fighting determination of about eight hundred Continental soldiers who fought the campaign's first close-quarter combat with the cream of Burgoyne's army. The Americans under Warner and Francis would give a good account of themselves at Hubbardton; they might have averted an even greater debacle for St. Clair and his retreating army.

As Fraser was meeting the rebels head to head near the crest of Monument Hill, the remainder of Grant's command was hard pressed at Sucker Brook. It appeared that Carr's New Hampshire men would turn their right flank. Fraser called for Acland's grenadiers to shore up the dead Grant's faltering

A British grenadier. *Courtesy of the New-York Historical Society.*

platoons and protect the British right flank. The hard-drinking Acland would lead a charmed warrior's life in the colonies only to die of a cold following a chilly morning duel back in England, a year later. Acland was also a politician back home. He had no love lost in his heart for the rebel cause. He meant to give the revolutionaries a good thrashing that day. Acland and his grenadiers came running to help Grant's struggling boys and add some beefy support to the right flank.[94]

Acland rushed to form his battalion for the push to save Fraser's right flank. As he did, one young grenadier officer had some trepidations about the fight he was about to enter. Lieutenant William Digby of the Fifty-third Foot later truthfully confided to his journal that "this being the first serious engagement I had ever been in, I must own, when we received orders to prime and load, which we barely had time to do before we received a heavy fire, the idea of perhaps a few moments conveying me before the presence of my Creator had its force." Digby did not allow his anxiety to get the best of him. He reconciled himself to whatever fate he would face. Anticipating that others would someday read his scribbling, Digby added, "Let not the reader imagine of my deviating at the time from my duty as a soldier, as I have always made it a rule that a proper resignation to the will of the Divine Being is the certain foundation for true bravery." Digby's age is a mystery, but he entered the army in 1770 as an ensign, so he probably was no more than twenty-two or twenty-three years old at the time.[95] His haunting words likely reflected the thoughts of many young men—officers and common soldiers, redcoats and Patriots—on the battlefield that day at Hubbardton.

Fraser's orders to Major Acland were to first secure the British right flank and then to prevent the Americans, if possible, from "gaining the road, which leads to Castleton and Skenesborough." Acland would carry out this assignment beyond his commander's expectations and change the course of the battle before the Germans arrived. Meanwhile, Fraser and the light infantry gained the crest of Monument Hill, which pushed the rebels back to "a hill of lower eminence which was their original post." Fraser was referring to the plateau portion of Monument Hill where the Patriots' regiments had camped the previous night. There is a slight rise in the ground on the southern end of Monument Hill that fits Fraser's description. The Castleton road also bisects this part of Monument Hill. The Americans would "for some hours maintain their ground, and endeavoured to surround us," one British officer told his journal. The battle on the Monument Hill plateau would be a seesaw contest, much to Major Lindsay's surprise. The earl later recalled that the rebels "certainly behaved with great gallantry." It would be here that the heaviest fighting would occur and the tide of battle would change.[96]

By the time Fraser and Lindsay's light infantrymen had gained Monument Hill, Acland's grenadier companies and remnants of Grant's Twenty-fourth Foot had swept over the camp of stragglers and disabled men in the bottomland below Monument Hill. The British captured several hundred prisoners. The Twenty-fourth Foot's battalion companies came in on Lindsay's right flank as Acland's grenadiers moved farther to the right, using the Mount Independence–Hubbardton military road as a guide. Captain Carr's New Hampshire company was swept aside or fled along with its regimental commander, Colonel Hale, who was no help to Warner in this fight. Hale's performance on July 7 would later be questioned and lead to charges of misconduct.

It was at this point that a very engaging, yet questionable, story is told by Thomas Anburey. It bears repeating with the caveat that it is highly suspect. To prove that the rebels were despicable characters, Anburey describes a surrender scene that allegedly occurred in the bottomland south of Sucker Brook. Two grenadier companies on the far right flank of Fraser's command noticed about sixty Americans walking toward them with their muskets clubbed—the traditional sign of surrender for eighteenth-century soldiers. Acland's grenadiers held their fire, allowing the rebels to get closer. When the faux prisoners got within ten yards of the enemy, they quickly reversed their muskets and fired a deadly volley at the unsuspecting British. Then the contemptible Americans instantly ran into the nearby woods. A number of grenadiers were killed and wounded. Those who remained pursued the rebels and "gave no quarter." Several well-known studies of Burgoyne's campaign have included Anburey's fanciful story. An Anburey critic makes a good case for questioning the volunteer officer when he concludes that "it is hard to imagine how, in the heat of battle, [the rebels] could have organized and timed this ruse; it is harder to imagine professional British soldiers letting their guard down so completely."[97]

It was now up to Warner's depleted Green Mountain regiment to block Acland's charging grenadiers who were bent on capturing the Castleton road and turning the American left flank. How the British grenadiers managed to gain the road and outflank Warner's left has been a matter of controversy and perhaps misinterpretation ever since.

6

THE PATH UP ZION HILL
LEADS TO DECEPTION

To understand the battle of Hubbardton, one must consider to what extent Zion Hill—or, as it is popularly called today, Mount Zion—factored into Fraser's or, for that matter, Warner's tactics. Hubbardton, unlike many Revolutionary War and Civil War battlefields, has not been compromised by latter-day development. It is a pristine location where one can get a real sense of what happened there on July 7, 1777. Standing on the southwest brow of Monument Hill, or virtually anywhere on the battlefield, one can easily see that Mount Zion is an impressive formation. It dominates the landscape, not only because of its 1,100-foot elevation but also because of its unique geological features. Its eastern face displays a rocky escarpment that beckons modern-day hikers whose only accoutrements may be a nylon backpack to carry a camera, perhaps binoculars, a water bottle, some fruit and granola bars. These twenty-first-century trampers, unlike Acland's husky grenadiers, are unencumbered by a heavy wool uniform, leather shoes with gaiters, a ten-pound "Brown Bess" musket, sixty rounds of ammunition in a leather cartridge box, a sixteen-inch bayonet, a haversack and a wooden canteen all held together with a web of belts and buckles.

Despite its terrain dominance, the question arises: was Mount Zion a factor in the battle on July 7? Depending on the answer, one could also ask: did the British use Mount Zion to outflank Warner's position south of the Selleck cabin and gain control of the Castleton road? These are important

Modern-day view of Mount Zion looking southwest from Monument Hill. *Author's collection.*

questions to ponder because anyone who wants to understand what happened at Hubbardton must consider the importance of Mount Zion. On the other hand, Mount Zion might have been irrelevant to the battle. Mount Zion might have had no impact on the tactics used by Brigadier Fraser or his counterpart, Colonel Warner. Still, anyone who writes about the battle must consider this terrain feature. Before continuing the story of Fraser's attack on the Americans, we must analyze the value of Mount Zion from a number of perspectives.

Most historians writing about the battle of Hubbardton rely on contemporary accounts written by participants or men who were serving in the campaign who heard stories from their comrades a few days later. This is the standard approach of historical inquiry when constructing a fact-supported narrative—use the letters, diaries, journals and reports of the soldiers who were there. These primary documents, whether published or in manuscript form, provide the best tool for retelling a story. When these documents are sparse, postwar memoirs or reminiscences can sometimes fill in the gaps.

But in the case of Hubbardton, some of these primary sources can be misleading or they can be misinterpreted. A classic example is the use of Thomas Anburey's *Travels through the Interior Parts of America*, published in

1789. From its first release, Anburey's accounts were questioned by reviewers. It seems he lifted material from other authors—a term commonly called plagiarism. A 1943 study exposed Anburey's inaccuracies in great detail. Twenty years later, even the editor of a new version of Anburey's account admitted to discrepancies but opted to overlook them. However, Anburey tells a great story, so writers are drawn to his words like moths to a light bulb.[98]

For example, Hoffman Nickerson's classic 1928 account of the 1777 campaign entitled *The Turning Point of the Revolution; or, Burgoyne in America* has Acland's physically large grenadiers scaling Mount Zion. Apparently, Nickerson, an army staff officer in both world wars and a prolific author of history books, questioned Lieutenant Anburey's personal account of the grenadiers climbing up Pittsford Ridge to gain Warner's rear. Nickerson liked the idea of putting Acland's troops up and over Mount Zion, the 1,100-foot-high rocky outcropping about a half mile southwest of the main battlefield. But did Nickerson's new interpretation make sense?

In 1960, the Vermont Board of Historic Sites requested Colonel Richard Dupuy, another military man who served on General Eisenhower's staff, to take another look at the Hubbardton battle. His research generated an unpublished study entitled "The Battle of Hubbardton: A Critical Analysis." Dupuy fell into the trap set by Nickerson. Dupuy believed Simon Fraser immediately recognized the tactical importance of Mount Zion. The British commander saw that "the key to complete victory lay on that craggy knob on the right front." Dupuy's opinion was valued, and a battlefield map designed specifically for the visitor's center has Major Acland's men using Mount Zion to reach their goal—Warner's rear and the Castleton road. A more recent commentator glibly remarks, "Today one large map showing the grenadiers' supposed sweep across Mount Zion remains in the visitor's center…although it hangs in an out of the way corner of the entrance hall."[99]

The idea of sturdy, red-coated grenadiers ascending Mount Zion was revisited by another army officer, Colonel John Williams, a veteran of World War II and Korea. Williams's research resulted in the publication of his 1988 monograph on the battle entitled *The Battle of Hubbardton: The American Rebels Stem the Tide*. Williams discounted previous assumptions that Acland used Mount Zion to outflank his opponents. Instead, Williams decided to reinterpret Anburey. He used Anburey's account to put the grenadiers back on Pittsford Ridge, which now became crucial to Fraser's tactical victory. The retired officer had the right interpretation of Hubbardton as a classic rear guard action that went awry for Warner when an overly aggressive British pursuer, Simon Fraser, did not follow Warner's plan.

But Williams's use of Anburey allowed his narrative to place too much emphasis on Pittsford Ridge. While Pittsford Ridge is certainly not as high as Mount Zion, it still would have been difficult for Acland's battalion to maintain the type of eighteenth-century line formation commonly used by the British army. At the start of the battle, Acland was leading only about 350 disciplined grenadiers and probably fewer than that by the time he would have approached Pittsford Ridge. These men were expected to move in tight formations, not like the famous rangers Major Robert Rogers commanded during the French and Indian War. It is difficult to see how Acland could have kept his grenadiers in line formation from the Castleton road to Pittsford Ridge without creating large gaps in his line. There were just not enough men to do it. However, Williams's viewpoint is the standard interpretation of the battle used by the state site today.[100] A different interpretation of what Acland might have done at Hubbardton will be discussed later in this narrative.

Despite Williams's efforts to change the perception away from Mount Zion as a pivotal feature of the battle, some historians and writers went right back to Anburey in subsequent studies. Perhaps the most popular book published to date on Burgoyne's 1777 campaign is *Saratoga: Turning Point of America's Revolutionary War*, written by respected author Richard Ketchum in 1997. Ketchum was no stranger to Revolutionary War topics. Before tackling Burgoyne's campaign, he wrote books on Bunker Hill and the battles of Trenton and Princeton. One comment on the dust jacket of his *Saratoga* book claimed, "His narrative is decisive, absolutely reliable, and wonderfully vivid." There is no question that Ketchum's excellent work on the 1777 campaign is still the standard. It is an elegantly written book using well-documented sources for his arguments. But in Ketchum's narrative on Hubbardton, Anburey's words are evident. The grenadiers fight for possession of a "rocky precipice that commanded the road to Castle Town," and they "haul themselves up the rocky face, clinging to bushes and bracing their feet on the branches of trees." These are delightful word pictures for the reader but probably not very accurate. Neither is Ketchum's conclusion that Acland's men ran down Mount Zion to capture the Castleton road and block Warner's planned retreat route. Interestingly, Ketchum's battlefield map of Hubbardton in his book has Lindsay's light infantry making a flank attack over the northern end of Mount Zion.[101]

Since Ketchum's book was released, at least four other studies of Burgoyne's campaign have been published. Three of these works include a reference to Acland's grenadiers and Mount Zion in one form or other. Brendan Morrissey's short but well-illustrated monograph entitled *Saratoga*

1777: Turning Point of a Revolution claims, "Fraser ordered Acland to climb Zion Hill, which commanded the road." Morrissey has the grenadiers near the mountain but not actually climbing over it. He describes other incidents that indicate he relied on Anburey as a source, but he has Acland seizing the Castleton road without running down Mount Zion to do it.[102]

In 2008, John F. Luzader's work entitled *Saratoga: A Military History of the Decisive Campaign of the American Revolution* again went back to Anburey for a description of what happened on the British right flank, perhaps influenced by Nickerson. Luzader was a longtime staff historian with the National Park Service and former historian at the Saratoga battlefield park. According to Luzader, "Major John Acland's battalion of grenadiers approached Zion Hill in a move intended to turn the Americans left and interdict an American retreat via the road to Castleton." Furthermore, Luzader wrote, "Warner's ploy…failed to halt the grenadiers, who slung their muskets and clawed their way up Zion's rocky slope, grabbing bushes and trees as they pulled themselves to the summit." Luzader has Acland wounded in the thigh on Mount Zion before his men "rushed down the reverse slope toward Warner's left flank and the road to Castleton." The battle map in Luzader's book clearly shows Acland coming up and over Mount Zion. Following on Luzader's study was Michael O. Logusz's *With Musket & Tomahawk: The Saratoga Campaign and the Wilderness War of 1777*, published in 2010. Logusz fell into Nickerson's trap too. His straightforward narrative had Acland's grenadiers climbing Mount Zion as Logusz tapped into the timeworn descriptions used by previous writers without considering the logic of Mount Zion's elevation and distance from the combat.

The most recent study of Burgoyne's campaign only spends about three pages discussing Hubbardton. Theodore Corbett's *No Turning Point: The Saratoga Campaign in Perspective*, published in 2012, forsakes the use of Anburey based on the convincing arguments made by Ennis Duling. Corbett writes a limited tactical description of the battle. He has the British light infantry move around a hill, "cutting off the possibility of the rebels escaping to Castleton." Corbett does not mention the name of the hill, but within the context of his narrative it is pretty clear that he means Monument Hill, not Mount Zion or Pittsford Ridge.[103]

Students of the battle of Hubbardton, or for any battle for that matter, should realize that there is no substitute for a personal investigation of the ground to test the logic of sources like Anburey. In modern military parlance, this would mean a "staff ride," where the written word is tested against existing geographic features like Mount Zion. A clear observation of the terrain at Hubbardton would reveal that there is plenty of room in the bottomland west of Monument Hill to maneuver a battalion of grenadiers without ordering them to climb Mount Zion. The Mount Independence military road funnels through a gap between Monument Hill and the lower portions of Mount Zion. As one commentator has concluded, "The supposed exploits on Mount Zion never made sense." In other words, "a trek over the mountain would have been a long, arduous, and pointless detour."[104] Major Acland never went near, up, over or down Mount Zion, but some British troops might have climbed a small hill that Anburey confused with Zion Hill as he was writing down his thoughts after the engagement.

ACLAND'S GRENADIERS
TO THE RESCUE

Once Acland's grenadiers joined the fight, right next to what was left of the Twenty-fourth Foot's battalion companies, it was too much for the Americans to withstand. The Patriots in the valley along Sucker Brook were a collection of troops from various commands. No doubt there were difficult command and control issues for the officers in that sector. In the valley, there was part of Hale's Second New Hampshire, perhaps some mixed companies from Francis's rear guard and, of course, the sick, disabled and stragglers picked up along the twenty-plus-mile retreat from Mount Independence. As one study of the battle contends, "The action [at Sucker Brook] was successful [from the American viewpoint] since the British deployed right and left of the crossing, a time consuming maneuver for British troops of that period." The Americans might have slowed the redcoats briefly, but they were no match for Acland's grenadiers.

It is unclear exactly how long these Americans made a stand, but it was probably less than a half hour after Grant was killed. The rebels broke and fled to the south and southwest, where they found some protection by the height of a nearby wooded hillside. Some of Francis's men might have made it back up the south slope of Monument Hill to rejoin the colonel near the Castleton road. Most of the Americans did not make it, however. Acland's battalion was halted south of Sucker Brook while the major gathered up what amounted to several hundred prisoners, mostly

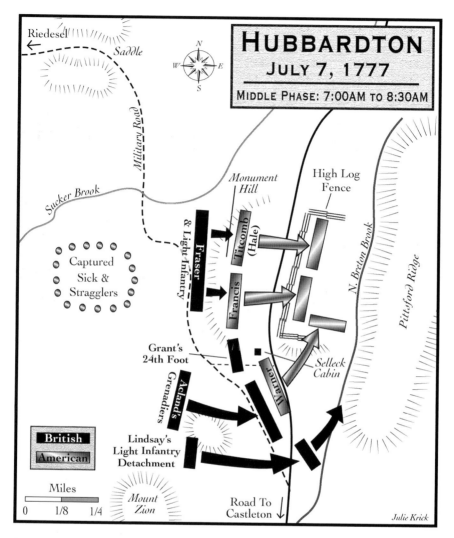

A map of the middle phase: 7:00 a.m. to 8:30 a.m. *Prepared by Julie Krick for the author.*

the sick, disabled and men who could have cared less about serving in the ranks.[105]

The limited stand the Americans made south of Sucker Brook bought time for Warner, who now deployed his Green Mountain regiment, or what was left of it, from a column of march on the Castleton road to a ragged line of battle. This maneuver might have caused Fraser to detach two light infantry companies under Lindsay to lead Acland's grenadiers around Monument Hill. "The light infantry detachment provided the speed required to reach and

A modern-day view of the south slope of Monument Hill. The roof of the Hubbardton Battlefield Visitor's Center is visible in the background. *Author's collection.*

outflank the rebels at the Castleton road," according to an army officer who studied Fraser's tactics at Hubbardton. If Fraser's report is a good indicator of what was happening on the battlefield, he seems to have lost contact with Acland's battalion at this point. Once he ordered the grenadiers to reinforce Grant, protect the British right and, if possible, gain the Castleton road, Fraser is silent on Acland's movements. The brigadier's only comment is that his "left was much weakened by this manouvre [*sic*]." Fraser's main concern now was his dependence on "the arrival of the Brunswick troops."[106]

The terrain south of Sucker Brook allowed Lindsay's two light infantry companies, which were leading Acland's grenadiers, to gain the Castleton road without climbing Mount Zion. There is a much smaller hill, unnamed even today, that lies east of Mount Zion and west of the military road before the 1776 road intersects with the Castleton road. It is possible that Lindsay's light infantry, and even some of Acland's grenadiers, used this lower hill as a way to gain the Castleton road. If the redcoats ascended this hill in an effort to intercept the Castleton road, then it is possible that this is where Anburey got his picture of troops going up a hill. Such a view could easily have been embellished by the young officer's imagination. Some of Lindsay's light troops could have even skirted this hill, without climbing it, as they attempted to get to the Castleton road.

Most of Acland's troops, however, would have spread out on both sides of the military road as they marched around the southern end of Monument Hill. Even the southwest corner of Monument Hill provides a steep enough slope to create a difficult climb. If any grenadiers tried to climb this slope, they would have had a difficult time. With a very limited number of firsthand accounts of the action on this part of the battlefield, it is hard to pinpoint whether or not the grenadiers or the light infantry did any climbing at all. Since it is fairly easy to see that Mount Zion was not a factor in the British movements, on the other hand, it is not farfetched to consider the British troops circling around the lower, unnamed hill. Such a maneuver would put them near the military road. This terrain feature—the lower, unnamed hill—could have been used, therefore, to the advantage of the redcoats.

Warner's Green Mountain Continentals, probably situated in the thalweg between the southern slope of Monument Hill and the lower hill farther south, were pushed back beyond the Castleton road by the weight of Acland's grenadiers. Warner's men most likely retreated to high ground opposite the Selleck cabin on the south end of Monument Hill and east of the Castleton road. The ground here rises sharply. This location gave the Vermonters a good defense position—at least temporarily. It also allowed Warner to refuse his left flank.

Once the grenadiers and Lindsay's light infantry detachment gained the road, there was no chance for the Americans to retreat south on the road to Castleton—a highway escape was effectively cut off. Fraser's order to send in his reserve—the ten grenadier companies—also strengthened the troops formerly under Grant that now were to the right of the light infantry companies under the brigadier. Williams has concluded, "This was a brilliant maneuver, and one of the keys to the British's eventual success. The envelopment not only sealed the road but continued across it to the northeast for one-half mile to the summit of Pittsford."[107]

Here is where Williams accepts Anburey's account in which the grenadiers gain the top of Pittsford Ridge. Anburey, however, might have appropriated language from Burgoyne's report to Lord Germain for his recollections of events. These memories were published twelve years after the battle. Only four days after the battle, Burgoyne sent a glowing letter to London of his campaign exploits from the time his army reached Crown Point until it reunited at Skenesborough. With regard to the engagement at Hubbardton, the commanding general stated that the Americans "attempted a retreat by Pittsford Mountain, but the Grenadiers scrambled up what had appeared

A modern-day view of the west side of Pittsford Ridge from Monument Hill near the Selleck cabin site. *Author's collection.*

an inaccessible part of the ascent and gained the Summit before them. This threw [the Americans] into confusion." There is little chance that Burgoyne, who was not on the field, of course, received his information from Anburey.

Most likely, Burgoyne was given a verbal report from his subordinate, Simon Fraser, which he incorporated into his letter to Germain. In the brigadier's own written account, he states that "when [the Americans] wished to gain the Castleton road by filing off to their left, they were met by the Granadiers [*sic*] who obliged them to attempt a retreat by scrambling up Huberton [*sic*] mountain [i.e. Pittsford Ridge], and march toward Pittsford falls." The movement Fraser is referring to might have occurred as that portion of the British light infantry under Fraser's direct command was pushing the rebels off the "hill of less eminence." The hill of "less eminence" was part of the Monument Hill plateau (near the present-day visitor's center). The grenadiers smashed into the Americans, pushing them back beyond the Castleton road to a defensive position behind a high log fence. It was during this attack that Major Acland might have been wounded. He was wounded in the thigh at Hubbardton, but the location where he was hit is speculative. No primary account describes the place where he went down. Since the fighting was heavy in this sector, it is not unreasonable to assume a musket ball wounded him here as his grenadiers attacked the southern end of Monument Hill.

Fraser further points out that "the Granadiers [sic] moved on the right of the enemy, and we got possession of the top of this hill before they could." This statement led Williams to believe that Acland's grenadiers got behind the Patriots, that is, on the Americans' right flank. Williams is probably in error with this assumption. By taking Fraser's words literally, it would mean the grenadiers came up on Titcomb's flank, since he was on the right of the American line as it faced Fraser. No German source mentions grenadiers in this sector. It is more plausible to assume that the British grenadiers were moving to their own right or Warner's left, which would threaten the American rear, rather than being in the Patriots' rear. Williams also assumes that Anburey was confirming Fraser's account when it is clear from evidence presented above that Anburey copied from other sources to create his own descriptions.[108]

In his analysis, Williams fails to consider the numbers involved. At the start of the battle, Acland probably had no more than 375 grenadiers. Lindsay's detachment of light infantry, assigned by Fraser to lead the grenadiers, would number perhaps another 75 troops. This estimate is before either command sustained any casualties in the Sucker Brook valley and the ascent up Monument Hill before the light infantry companies were detached.

There is an open field south of Monument Hill between the Castleton road and North Breton Brook to the east. Beyond the east side of the creek, Pittsford Ridge starts a slow ascent to its spine. The field is approximately two hundred yards wide from the road to the creek. If the grenadier battalion was formed in two ranks across this field, there would be barely enough men to extend much beyond North Breton Brook. More likely, some of Lindsay's more agile light infantrymen crossed the creek and scrambled up the lower slope of Pittsford Ridge, giving Warner concern that his left would be flanked. Although Fraser refers to "Granadiers" in his report, he was nowhere near the action on this part of the field. If there were red-coated soldiers on Pittsford Ridge, they were most likely Lindsay's light infantrymen and not a large number of them. An unidentified officer in the Forty-seventh Foot gives a clue to this scenario. In his campaign journal, this officer records that the Americans were cut off in their retreat "by the last of the Lt. infantry and part of the Grenadiers, who gained the summet [sic]."[109] This observation appears to verify that there was a small contingent of light infantrymen and perhaps some grenadiers east of the creek on the ridge, but certainly not a grenadier battalion. There were enough redcoats on the ridge, however, for Warner to see them, which forced him to start considering new options.

HARD FIGHTING ON MONUMENT HILL

The bloodiest action of the day was happening on Monument Hill. Fraser immediately recognized the military importance this commanding hill had on the deployment of his troops at the start of the battle. According to his report, after sending Grant's advance guard down the military road toward Sucker Brook and the valley area, Fraser himself stayed with Lindsay's light infantry battalion, facing them to the left for a frontal assault on the west side of the hill. Fraser's boys gained the crest of the hill as Warner ordered parts of Francis's rear guard and Titcomb's New Hampshire regiment to advance from the Castleton road where they were in column ready to depart from Hubbardton. It appears that these troops hit Fraser at the crest of Monument Hill or slightly below it. No matter the exact location, Fraser's light infantrymen with the brigadier running with them had an unstoppable momentum that pushed the Americans back as the British gained the top of the hill.

At this point, the Americans were pushed back to the "hill of less eminence, which was their original post" where they rallied. Williams identifies the "hill of less eminence" as being behind the high log fence. But the log fence was east of the Castleton road. It is more likely that after they were pushed by Fraser's light infantrymen from the eastern crest of Monument Hill, the Americans took up a second position on a rise west of the road (near the back of the present-day visitor's center). The Americans might have tried a counterattack against the British from this ground before retreating, but it

British troops in the foreground depict a battle scenario at the 2014 annual reenactment at the Hubbardton Battlefield Site. *Author's collection.*

is difficult to prove from existing sources. It does seem clear that the rebels were not able to hold this position long before they were pushed beyond the road and formed behind the high log fence.[110]

Despite his success, Fraser still was looking for "the arrival of the Brunswick troops," although he had sent several messages back to Riedesel to hasten his men to Hubbardton. The redcoats furiously continued their attack down the east slope of Monument Hill to where the ground rises again just west of the Castleton road. The rebels "were pushed so warmly here, that they left it," according to Fraser. At this point, the Americans might have attempted a retreat south along the road near the Selleck cabin only to face Acland's grenadiers who had come up through the draw at the southern end of Monument Hill along the spur of the military road below the cabin. As Fraser reports, "When [the Americans] wished to gain the Castleton road, by filing off to their left, they were met by the Granadiers [*sic*] who obliged them to retreat."[111]

The famous Vermont revolutionary Ethan Allen (who was not present at Hubbardton) later claimed that "the enemy advanced boldly, and the two bodies formed within 60 yards of each other. Col. Warner having formed his own regiment, and that of Col. Francis did not wait for the enemy, but gave them a heavy fire from his whole line; and they returned it with great bravery." Allen added, "The enemy broke, and gave way on the right and left, but formed again, and renewed the attack." Meanwhile, according to Allen, Acland's grenadiers, whom he placed "in the centre [sic] of the enemy's line, maintained the ground, and finally carried it with the point of the bayonet, and Warner retreated with resolution." Some of Allen's information is very specific and basically reflects what happened between Fraser's light infantrymen and the Americans fighting on the Monument Hill plateau. His account is interesting because he claims the opposing forces were sixty yards apart. Based on the heavy British casualties at Hubbardton, this range makes sense. Each side was using muskets with a killing range of eighty yards; therefore, Allen's account seems credible. Allen is the only source that has British bayonets employed to rout the Americans. But again, this was a standard tactic of the British army, used particularly by the heavy troops. And it was intimidating.[112]

Does Ethan Allen's account have credibility based on the fact that he wasn't at the battle? There is no way to know for sure how Allen got his information about Hubbardton. However, if he was Seth Warner's cousin, as one writer claims, it is possible that Allen's description of the battle reflects a later conversation between Allen and Warner, despite their earlier rift over command of the Green Mountain regiment.[113] Based on the dimensions of the Monument Hill plateau, it is easy to visualize the two sides blasting away at sixty yards apart.

Now Warner's command, or what was left of it anyway, rallied behind a high log fence that was part of farmer Selleck's cornfield. It was here that Warner bought crucial time for St. Clair at the expense of his own command. Fraser's boys made it hot for Warner in what one British officer later claimed "was such a fire sent amongst them as not easily conceived."[114]

St. Clair had not forgotten about his rear guard even though he was not happy with Warner for staying an extra night at Hubbardton. "The moment the firing was heard in Castle-Town, the General determined to support the rear guard at Hubbardton," Major Henry Brockholst Livingston testified at St. Clair's court-martial a year after the battle. When St. Clair's courier returned from delivering the bad news about Skenesborough to Warner and his subordinates, the army commander found out more about the unavoidable fight at Hubbardton. The prospect of close combat with the British at this time did not enthuse St. Clair, who wanted to move at once to Rutland. St. Clair's goal was to transfer the burden of army command to his departmental boss, Schuyler, not engage Burgoyne's army. Nevertheless,

St. Clair immediately dispatched two aides to Ransomvale to urge the militia units closest to Warner to march to his relief. St. Clair's main army at Castleton was ready to march to Rutland but was ordered to wait until more information came in from Warner.[115]

Livingston and Major Isaac Dunn quickly mounted their horses and galloped the three miles from Castleton to Ransomvale, where the recalcitrant militia regiments had encamped the previous night. Livingston was an aide de camp to General Schuyler, while Dunn served St. Clair. Colonel Benjamin Bellows commanded the two Massachusetts militia regiments. Livingston and Dunn had orders from St. Clair that told Bellows to march immediately with his two regiments to the relief of Colonel Francis. It's interesting to note that Francis is mentioned by the aide rather than Warner, perhaps representing a pique on St. Clair's part. The two aides were to assure Bellows that if he ran into trouble, the main army would be there to support him. Livingston and Dunn never made it to Ransomvale, but they were able to deliver the orders to Bellows.

While riding toward Ransomvale, the two aides spotted Bellows and his two militia regiments marching "with speed" south toward Castleton, rather than being camped at Ransomvale. As Livingston later testified, "We delivered our orders, but could not prevail upon either regiment to reinforce the rear guard." Livingston had to admit that Bellows was not to blame because the colonel was actually in the rear of his command, which means he was closer to Hubbardton than the rest of his men. Bellows had "warmly persuaded them to go to the field of action," but "an unaccountable panic had seized his men, and no commands or intreaties [sic] had any effect on them." With their mission in shambles, the two brave young aides decided to ride farther north to see what was happening at Hubbardton. This way they could give an eyewitness report to St. Clair.[116]

Dunn and Livingston had not ridden very far when they met Captain Chadwick with about thirty men marching south from Hubbardton. Chadwick was the bearer of bad news. There would be no need for reinforcements. The action at Hubbardton was over. Warner's rear guard had dispersed. The captain's advice was to not go near the battlefield, unless Dunn and Livingston wanted to risk capture by the British. Despite their youth, the two aides were smart enough not to try something so foolhardy, even if it sounded exciting. They pulled their horses' reins and galloped as fast as they could to Castleton. The only thing the aides could report to their commander was that Warner had ordered his men to rally at Manchester, so they could fight another day.[117]

As Livingston and Dunn negotiated with Bellows's militiamen, Warner retreated to the rise formed on the southern end of Monument Hill on the east side of the Castleton road. He would place what men were left in his Green Mountain regiment and those who had joined him from the Sucker Brook retreat behind a high log fence.

The perimeter formed by the log fence was shaped like a long inverted "u." The left side of the fence formed a right angle above a sharp slope on the east side of Monument Hill heading away from the Castleton road. It was here that Warner's Green Mountain troops rallied after running into Acland's grenadiers and the light infantry that formed Fraser's right. These troops had come up through the draw where the military road intersected with the Castleton road, forcing Warner to give ground. The right side of the log fence also formed a right angle, which partially protected the right flank of Titcomb's command. Titcomb's line might have extended beyond the angle of the log fence. Unfortunately, both the left and right sides of the fence did not extend very far. The section of the fence that faced the Castleton road was significantly longer than either of its sides. However, the entire log fence gave the Americans enough protection that they were able to put up a stout defense where, according to one British officer, "they for some hours maintained their ground." Another redcoat officer, Joshua Pell, described the rebel position formed "behind enclosures, which in this Country are compos'd of large Trees, laid one upon the other and make a strong breastwork." In his order book dated three days after the battle, General Burgoyne also mentioned that the "rebels were strongly fortified" and "long defended themselves by the aid of logs and trees."[118]

One American participant named Joseph Bird recalled many years after the battle that his company commander, Captain Stone, "removed the three top rails, for seven or eight lengths, so that we could have a better chance at them." Bird also claimed the Patriots "drove them back twice, by cutting them down so fast." He was near the center of the American line where Francis commanded. The new defensive position behind the log fence was a magnetized barrier for the Americans. "We didn't leave [the] log fence or charge them," Bird remembered. The young soldier claimed to have "fired 20 cartridges" during this shootout with the redcoats at the log fence. As Williams surmises, "Francis absorbed the main British assault, and his command, which included the original rear guard, provided the strongest opposition."[119]

Fraser's light infantrymen on the left of the British battle line had charged up Monument Hill, met Francis and his Continentals somewhere near the crest or slightly below it, pushed them back and continued to

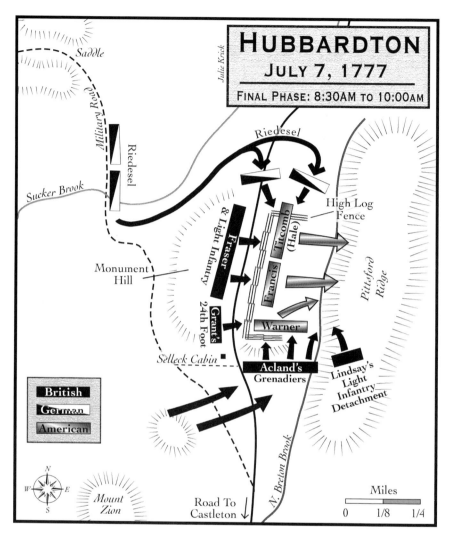

A map of the final phase: 8:30 a.m. to 10:00 a.m. *Prepared by Julie Krick for the author.*

attack the rebel line. When they debouched from the Mount Independence military road, the light infantry battalion counted perhaps 375 men. Now, they had been in heavy combat for over an hour, and the casualties were mounting. Once Fraser gained the crest of the hill, he continued down the eastern slope, pushing Francis's and Titcomb's troops back to the "hill of lower eminence." The Americans may have counterattacked in the area below the slope of Monument Hill or from the lower elevation west of the Castleton road before retreating behind the high log fence where they made a stout defense. All of this maneuvering and volley fire had somewhat disorganized Fraser's companies.

The Americans realized the weakness of Fraser's left. The Patriots now made an effort to turn the British left flank. As the brigadier recalled, the Americans "made some demonstrations to renew the attack," which "they began pretty briskly." This turning movement is chiefly attributed to Titcomb and the portion of the Second New Hampshire Regiment he commanded to Francis's right. The reconnaissance party of two hundred men sent out by Warner might have also joined in this attack. Fraser refers to "a party that was desirous to gain the road from Huberton [*sic*] toward the lower part of Otter Creek by Chimney point observed the weakness of my left." Admittedly, Fraser's account is confusing, but Warner's scouting party probably used the old Crown Point military road, which originated near Chimney Point opposite the fort at Crown Point. Other chroniclers of the battle have not pointed out this possibility.

Williams attributes the American decision to hit Fraser's left to a fear that the rebels would be "trapped in a virtual cul-de-sac" if they remained behind the log fence. Francis and Titcomb would make one desperate attempt to give the Americans some breathing room so a disengagement could be initiated before the redcoats recovered from their last repulse. It seems from Bird's account, however, that the Patriots were comfortable behind their log fortification.

Reinforcements from the north, however, might have sparked the idea of the flanking movement. The returning scouting party, two hundred strong, might have provided the needed incentive to crush Fraser. This scenario is speculative, but it has some logic to it. The scouting party was supposed to return by 7:00 a.m. so Warner could depart Hubbardton. There is no mention of this unit returning before the action commenced—perhaps it was late. With Fraser's weakened left dangling in the air, the arrival of the scouting party on the American right provided the perfect opportunity for Titcomb to sally forth from his section of the log fence. The American attack on Fraser's exposed left was short-lived, however.[120]

9

BARON VON RIEDESEL
SAVES THE DAY

While Fraser was making his initial attack on Monument Hill about 7:30 a.m., Riedesel—with his advance guard of Jäger and grenadiers, about 180 men—was marching up the far side of Sargent Hill. More Germans would follow from Lacey's Camp, where the entire force had spent the night of July 6. In all, Riedesel had about 1,100 Brunswick infantrymen under his command. The German general was pushing his sweating troops in their heavy wool uniforms as quickly as he could because Fraser's most recent message carried an air of anxiety. The brigadier had apparently run into more than he could handle. He needed reinforcements—now! In the sparsely populated Vermont wilderness, sounds carried for miles. Riedesel undoubtedly heard the rattle of musketry as both Grant and Fraser ran into trouble. He urged his men forward along the tree-stumped military road, while at the same time sending Captain Poellnitz back with a message for Lieutenant Colonel Breymann, who was with the main body, to step up the pace. He sent another officer running up the road toward Hubbardton to reassure Fraser he was on his way.[121]

At about 8:15 a.m., Riedesel reached a clearing on Sargent Hill that gave him a commanding view of Monument Hill and the American effort to outflank Fraser's left. How Riedesel could see through the July foliage only becomes apparent if one accepts his reminiscences. It would have been very difficult for the nobleman to see this scene because Sargent Hill was mostly wooded at the time. Nevertheless, Riedesel wisely decided to attempt to outflank the flanking movement of the enemy. No matter what he saw or didn't see from Sargent Hill, the baron made the right decision. Once his exhausted Brunswickers had a few minutes to catch their breath after their hike up Sargent Hill, Riedesel issued orders for an advance on Monument Hill.[122]

His orders were for a classic envelopment maneuver of the American right flank by his Jäger company and his grenadiers. It was the type of tactic he learned on European battlefields. The one-hundred-man Jäger company would advance down the military road but turn sharply left. The Jäger would assault Monument Hill but farther north than Fraser's light infantrymen. The Jäger frontal attack would come up Monument Hill near where the old cemetery stands today. By turning sooner than Fraser, the Germans would be farther to the left of Fraser's line; it would also put them on the flank of Titcomb's regiment as they were attacking Fraser's left. Riedesel sent his grenadiers—about eighty soldiers—on a more circuitous route, which would put them in Titcomb's rear. Once the grenadiers reached the northern end of Monument Hill and crossed the Castleton road, they were to turn south. This trek would put them in the American rear, similar to what Lindsay's light infantrymen were doing on the rebel left. Riedesel would also add a ruse to his planned movements.[123]

To confuse the enemy into thinking the Germans were attacking with more men than they actually had on the field, Riedesel ordered his little German band to play. According to the general, the band actually preceded the Jäger in the attack. Not only did it fool the rebels, but the music inspired German and King's men alike. The Jäger joined the band by singing hymns to heighten morale. It was a well-formulated plan that was well executed, too. The band music and hymn singing also fooled a redcoat officer who claimed, "We were apprehensive, by the noise we heard, that a reinforcement had been sent back from the main body of the American army for the support of their rear guard." For added insurance, Riedesel sent another courier back to Breymann, urging him to quicken his pace. He also received another message from Fraser. The brigadier feared his left was surrounded. Riedesel reassured the Scotsman help was coming shortly. In fact, the German general demurred to Fraser, asking him through an aide how he would like to employ his troops. The Scotsman's concern about Riedesel taking over the battle was ill conceived. The baron would be a team player in this fight.[124]

Riedesel's Jäger company advanced under the command of Captain Carl von Geyso; they were met with a brisk resistance at first. The Brunswickers did not flinch but poured on a hot, deadly fire from their short-barreled rifles. When he felt the rebels were sufficiently softened up by the long-range accuracy of his riflemen, von Geyso ordered his Jäger to fix bayonets and advance against the enemy. Meanwhile, Captain Maximilian von Schottelius led his grenadiers to the far right of the American line so that they were nearly in their rear. A German grenadier later wrote, "When we arrived, we advanced as on a parade ground against the breastworks of the enemy. The rebels let us come within 50 paces of them, when they gave a general discharge, by which however we only had 4 killed and 6 wounded." This two-pronged assault from different directions by capable officers was more than the Patriots could stand. Titcomb's attack on Fraser faltered, and now his defensive line began to dissolve. Titcomb himself was hit by a German ball in his right shoulder, permanently disabling the major. Fraser's report claimed that it was a matter of minutes—six to be exact—before the enemy was thrown into retreat. Riedesel later remembered that it took twelve minutes to beat back the Americans and send them flying. No matter which account is right, it was not long before things were unraveling for Warner.[125]

THE DEATH OF COLONEL FRANCIS

It might have been at this point that Colonel Francis was killed. Throughout the engagement, the Massachusetts colonel was a bulwark for the American forces. He had led a masterful rear guard retreat from Mount Independence the previous day. He was up early with Warner, organizing a defensive position. He led his men from a column of march to stop Fraser cold on Monument Hill. He helped maintain the fallback position on the "hill of lower eminence" before finally pulling his troops back to the last stand at a high log fence. He surely walked back and forth in the rear of his men and their company commanders behind the log fence waiting for a chance to exploit a British tactical mistake. That chance came when Fraser allowed his left to be exposed. Titcomb and perhaps the returning scouting party jumped on the opportunity to attack the weakened light infantrymen. Fraser said this attack "began very briskly." But the sudden appearance of Riedesel, his Jäger, grenadiers, drums and brass band stymied the American attempt to flank Fraser. As the Patriots faltered under German firepower and the threat of the bayonet, Francis might have run to help the right side of the line.

The unreliable Anburey implies Francis fell somewhere on Pittsford Ridge because his personal papers were being read by Captain John Shrimpton, a grenadier in the Sixty-second Foot, on Pittsford Ridge when Shrimpton was shot down by a lingering rebel. Anburey does not specifically state where Francis's body was laying at the time his letters were read. The implication is that he was killed while retreating after the American line broke under pressure from the German flank attack.

Williams uses Joseph Bird's recollection to support Anburey's version of the colonel's death. According to the young Massachusetts soldier, "Col. Francis told me to take off my pack. I replied that I could fight with it on." Francis repeated his order to the stubborn youth. It makes sense that Francis would have told Bird to remove his pack if he was behind a defensive work of sorts. By this time, "smoke was so thick on the hill, we did not see the enemy until they fired. There being some scattering firing, Francis told his soldiers not to fire, they were firing on their own men. Then came a British volley and Francis fell dead." Bird's account can really be read more than one way. Bird mentions that smoke was pretty thick "on the hill" but does not identify which hill he is talking about. Williams chose to interpret Bird as meaning Pittsford Ridge. Bird could very well have been referring to Monument Hill. When Bird and Francis were fighting behind the log fence, they were still on Monument Hill. The fact that Francis could give orders to his soldiers belies the fact that there must have been some orderly arrangement for him to do it. Giving orders during a rout is rarely effective. In addition, Bird makes no reference to retreating. Smoke would have been heavy at the log fence as the British were pouring in volley after volley of musket fire on the Patriots hunkered down behind the fence; it probably would have been as thick as Bird described it. Francis's order to hold fire as not to shoot into their own men could indicate that he was watching Titcomb's flank attack, rather than shooting into retreating soldiers. Bird's account only makes sense if there was some kind of order left among the Americans as they retreated—a doubtful situation.

To bolster his argument that Anburey's account of Francis's death is the right one, Williams further relies on another eyewitness account from Captain Moses Greenleaf. This officer told his journal that "numbers fell on both sides, among ours the brave and ever to be lamented Col. Francis, who fought bravely to the last. He first received a ball through the right arm, but still continued at the head of our troops, till he received the fatal wound through his body, entering his right breast, he dropped on his face." Nowhere does Greenleaf mention the location where Francis went down. Getting hit in the chest for a man of Francis's courage would mean that he was facing the enemy, rather than retreating. Greenleaf's description, therefore, does not support Williams's conclusion that he died on Pittsford Ridge. Furthermore, Williams fails to include the rest of Greenleaf's narrative, which seems to indicate that Francis fell before the retreat started. The captain continues his account by saying, "Our people, being overpowered by numbers, were obliged to retreat over the mountain, enduring on their march great

The Hubbardton Battle Monument was erected in 1859 by the "Citizens of Hubbardton and Vicinity" to commemorate where "The Green Mountain Boys Fought Bravely." Tradition holds that Colonel Ebenezer Francis is buried under the monument. *Courtesy of Sandy Goss/Eagle Bay Media.*

privations and sufferings." When Greenleaf's full recollection is read, it seems to indicate that Francis died before the retreat over Pittsford Ridge started.

Likewise, Warner's nineteenth-century biographer, who claimed to have known the colonel as a youth, wrote that "Francis' regiment gave way, owing, as it afterward appeared, to the loss of their Colonel." If Francis had been killed on Pittsford Ridge, this would have been during the American retreat. It seems more likely, as pointed out by this writer, that the line collapsed after and because Francis went down. The colonel's death, therefore, precipitated the retreat up and over Pittsford Ridge.

Moreover, Williams does not use an additional Bird recollection that might further prove that Francis was not killed on Pittsford Ridge but instead died heroically on Monument Hill near the log fence. After Francis was killed, Bird remembered that "Capt. Hitchcook, one of our captains, came to me, and tried to speak, but as he had been wounded in the mouth, he could not [talk]." At that point, Bird continues, "Major Furnell of the 6th Mass. Regiment came up and told me they were surrounding us, and said 'make your escape.' I then took up my pack, by the straps and ran down the east side of the hill." Bird would lose his pack when it caught on "something" during his scamper to safety. This description, again, implies that Francis was killed before the retreat over Pittsford Ridge.

Ebenezer Francis was undoubtedly a hero at the battle of Hubbardton. More in keeping with Francis's character and leadership style is the scene created from Riedesel's memory. The Brunswick general remembered that Francis "fell, pierced by a German bullet, while leading the third attack on the left wing, and was buried by the Brunswick troops." A German diarist who was not at Hubbardton but might have heard camp talk afterward told his journal that Francis "was shot 7 times and killed." A British officer said that after Francis fell, the Americans "did not long stand," intimating that the rebels were in a fixed position (i.e. the log fence) rather than executing some type of retreating movement as implied by Anburey. Lieutenant Digby claimed to have seen Francis "after he fell, and his appearance caused me to remark his figure, which was fine & and even at that time made me regard him with attention." Another officer in the Forty-seventh Foot who was not on the scene at Hubbardton told his journal that "Col. Frances [*sic*] was left Dead on the Field," not on the wooded slope of Pittsford Ridge.[126]

THE PATRIOT LINE BREAKS

Riedesel's troops saved the day for Fraser, although a proud British officer told his journal with characteristic aplomb that "a party of Germans came up [in] time enough also *to share* [emphasis added] in the glory of the day, and the regular fire they gave at a critical time was material service to us." There would have been little glory to share if the Brunswickers had not arrived in the nick of time. Riedesel's Germans provided more than "material service" to the tottering British left flank. They virtually crushed the rebel flanking movement, causing the New Hampshire troops and others to abandon the battlefield—and quickly.[127]

Once their right flank and rear were compromised by the arrival of Riedesel's Germans, most Americans realized flight from the log fence was the best option. The threat of a gleaming bayonet charge by green-jacketed Jäger and blue-coated grenadiers was a very real possibility—and not something the New Englanders relished. One of the rebels who fled through a wheat field east of Monument Hill remembered how he "took a tree and waited for them to come within shot. We fought through the woods, all the way to the ridge of the Pittsford mountain, popping away from behind trees." This delaying tactic influenced a British lieutenant to tell his journal that the battle "lasted near three hours, before they attempted retreating, with great obstinacy."[128]

When Warner saw Francis's line give way, he knew the battle was lost. He lost his normally stoic equanimity and "poured out a torrent of execrations upon the flying troops." But with his right flank and rear crumbling under

American troops depict a battle scenario at the 2014 annual reenactment at the Hubbardton Battlefield Site. This event is held each year on the weekend closest to the battle's anniversary date. *Author's collection.*

pressure from Riedesel's Germans and Acland's grenadiers attacking his left with help from Lindsay's light infantry detachment as they reached the ridge, Warner regained his composure and yelled for his men to "scatter and meet me in Manchester."[129] This order precipitated a general rout of the rebels as they scrambled down the east side of Monument Hill and climbed up and over Pittsford Ridge. Except for some scattered sniping from behind trees on the ridge, the battle of Hubbardton was over. Fraser could finally breathe a sigh of relief.

A British officer remarked that the Americans "had two Colonels killed, one taken prisoner, with many other officers killed and taken prisoner." We know that Francis was killed and Colonel Hale was made a prisoner, but why would the Englishman think a second colonel was killed? Perhaps because a rumor floated around shortly after the battle that Seth Warner had, in fact, been shot down toward the end of the fight. But that's all it was—a rumor. When Warner heard the story a few days later, he was not surprised. "Being a moderate spoken man," he was not offended either because he could see how the mistaken impression happened in the heat of battle. As

Warner explained, toward the end of combat, he stood on a stump to get a better view of what was happening. One of his officers, who was sent to the American left flank to prevent the British grenadiers from outflanking the Patriots, gave the order to retreat, instead of advance. Warner doesn't say how the mistake was made, but the erroneous command turned the tide in favor of the British. The rebels needed no encouragement after almost three hours of intense fighting—they broke and ran. Warner ran over to prevent the rout but got his foot caught in a tree root or some other natural trap, causing the colonel to plunge into a "brush fence or heap." Warner's sudden fall gave the impression he was permanently down as the Americans fled from Monument Hill to the east. The humble Warner felt that if the mistaken order had not been shouted, the Patriots would have continued fighting and forced the British to give ground.[130] Whether Warner's story of falling headfirst on a tree root is true or not, his assessment of how the battle was going for the Americans is somewhat capricious. Notwithstanding any mistaken orders, it was pretty clear by mid-morning with Riedesel's arrival that Warner's rear guard would give way.

Hubbardton had been a hard fight for the British. By about 10:00 a.m., the heavy fighting was over, save for scattered sniping from a rebel or two. One of these stray shots wounded Captain Shrimpton, who jumped in the air, screaming he was hit. According to one source, the captain was standing with a group of officers supposedly reading some personal papers found on Colonel Francis's body when a ball whizzed into his shoulder. His comrades all knew it came from the wooded ridge to the east. A small detachment was sent to look for the would-be assassin but came back empty-handed. This sniping incident might have been the first example of *petite guerre* during Burgoyne's campaign. A small-scale, guerrilla-type warfare would later plague Burgoyne's army incessantly during late September and early October near Saratoga. It was unnerving to get shot at after the battle was over, especially for the British, but the Americans would later gain "absolute ascendency" in sniping and small skirmishing.[131]

It wasn't long after the firing ceased that the missing Colonel Nathan Hale showed his face. Where he had been for most of the action is still a mystery. Apparently Hale and about seventy men were surrounded after the action. They were captured by a ruse perpetrated on them by a clever unidentified redcoat officer. Lieutenant Hadden tells the story of how the unconventional surrender was accomplished: "As proof of what may be done against Beaten Battalions while their fears are upon them, an Officer and 15 Men detached for the purpose of bringing in Cattle fell in with 70 Rebels, affecting to have the rest of the party concealed and assuring them they were surrounded [by a larger number of regulars], they surrender'd their *Arms* [emphasis in the original] and were brought in [as] Prisoners."[132] Hale was among those captured in this manner.[133]

Although not present at the battle, Ethan Allen nevertheless chimed in later about Hale's surrender to "an inconsiderable number of the enemy." The notorious leader of the Green Mountain Boys wrote that Hubbardton "was by this time dangerous for those of both parties who were not prepared for the world to come." Allen said, "Col. Hale being apprised of the danger, never brought his regiment to the charge, but left Warner and Francis to stand the blowing of it, and fled, but luckily" was captured by the British and "to his eternal shame, surrendered himself a prisoner."[134] Allen does not reveal how he received his information about Hale's conduct, but perhaps it came from Seth Warner.

Hale was sent to Ticonderoga as a prisoner of war but released on parole two weeks later. He returned to his home in Rindge, New Hampshire, to await his exchange. In August 1777, when General Gates took command of the northern army from Schuyler, the new commanding officer immediately issued an order to arrest Hale on charges of treason, forwarding the directive to Major General Benjamin Lincoln, who was stationed in the Hampshire Grants at the time. Lincoln contacted the New Hampshire Committee of Safety, telling them Hale was wanted in Albany to answer Gates's charges. For whatever reason, Hale was never arrested and returned to British custody in June 1779 when his parole expired. He remained a prisoner of war until his death on September 23, 1780, at New Utrecht, Long Island.

The prolific sketch artist and amateur historian of the nineteenth century Benson Lossing, who visited the Hubbardton battlefield sometime during the 1840s, heard stories that gave him a different take on Hale's performance at Sucker Brook. Lossing wanted his readers to know another side of the story. He found that Hale and a large portion of his men were in poor health at the time of the battle. It's true that the colonel was assigned to guard the sick, disabled and stragglers by Warner. Lossing believed that Hale was actually unfit for service. Hale's retreat from the battlefield into the woods south of Sucker Brook was designed to save the sick men in his charge. Hale's action was "one of precaution rather than of cowardly alarm." It was supposedly Hale's New Hampshire rivals who circulated vicious rumors about his conduct at Hubbardton after he surrendered. These antagonists gave the wrong impression of the colonel's leadership. When Hale heard about these vile reports, he wrote to General

Washington asking to be exchanged. Once free, he could demand a court-martial, which Hale figured would clear his name. Unfortunately for Hale, he died before Washington acted on his request.[135]

Hale never had a chance to clear his name, if that would have been possible. "An unfortunate uncertainty hangs over" Hale, said one writer.[136] Why Gates decided on a charge of treason rather than cowardice in the face of the enemy is unclear from the existing record. The latter charge probably would have made more sense. However, no matter what the charge, Colonel Nathan Hale remains a footnote in history, while the better-known Nathan Hale is hailed as a national hero.

12

FRASER HOLDS THE FIELD

It had been nearly three hours of heavy fighting with horrific casualties sustained on both sides. Mopping up operations, in modern military vernacular, began as soon as the firing died down. For the British and Germans, it was time to tend to the wounded and count the dead. If Francis was beloved on the American side, Grant's death had a similar effect on Simon Fraser. As he expressed it in a letter to his friend John Robinson a few days after Hubbardton, the Scotsman said, "I feel very sensibly the death of Major Grant, no man was ever more attached to another than he was to me, & extremely useful to me on many occasions." Fraser was deeply affected by Major Grant's death, but he also expressed his feelings for his officers who were wounded. "I was rendered miserable by the sufferings of twelve respectable Gentlemen who were languishing under their wounds in a very unpleasant situation," he said.[137]

The brigadier had a right to feel bad; it was his own rashness in leaving Mount Independence without surgeons or medical supplies that contributed to the officers' suffering. But Fraser could not dwell on his feelings for long because as soon as the action ended, his practical concerns immediately became "dressing the wounded, burying the dead, and getting Bullocks to support the living." His soldiers started making bark huts to keep the wounded out of the burning sun. A torrential rain fell later in the day, lowering the temperature, but the suffering continued until relief came from the main army. Water was the men's only refreshment.[138]

By this time all of Riedesel's troops had arrived at Hubbardton to secure the flanks of Fraser's depleted command. The German general had Major

Ferdinand von Barner's Chasseurs, or light infantry battalion, deploy on the left to support Geyso's Jäger company and Schottelius's grenadiers. Major Otto von Mengen's grenadier battalion and Riedesel's own Braunschweiger Regiment were sent to the right to guard the Castleton road. Due to the food shortage at Hubbardton, "it was agreed that Riedesel should march to Skenesborough, and Fraser should remain where he was until orders had been received from Burgoyne in relation to the disposition of the wounded." The Germans left Hubbardton at noon on July 8 and reached Castleton that evening. They arrived in Skenesborough the next day at noon. When an astonished Fraser heard about the pace Riedesel's troops had set during the last twenty-four hours, he snarkily remarked, "[Riedesel] made a march rather more rapid than when he moved to my support." One of Fraser's officers observed "some little jealously between the two Generals"—an understatement to be sure.[139] Clearly the Scotsman was still smarting over the fact that the German general had saved his bacon but not soon enough for Fraser himself to lead the rout of the rebels.

Fraser was unable to move his command the next day, July 8, due to his lack of provisions and ammunition, so he put the able-bodied prisoners he had captured to work building log works to protect his regulars against a possible rebuttal attack by the rebels. His scouts brought in reports that the Americans "were gathering strength hourly." This caused Fraser concern because he felt he "was then in the most disaffected part of America" where every person was a spy. His worries were unnecessary; the rebels were high-tailing it to Manchester and Rutland, putting as much distance between themselves and the redcoats as possible.[140]

One advantage of staying around Hubbardton for an extra day was the plunder the redcoats retrieved from the dead, wounded and captured Americans—it turned out to be more than they could carry. A British officer wryly noted that there were "great quantities of paper money which was not the least regarded then, tho[ugh] had we kept it, it would have been of service, as affairs turned out." At two o'clock in the morning on July 9, Fraser had the rebel prisoners removed to Ticonderoga under a captain's guard of two grenadier companies.[141]

Later that same morning, Fraser roused his weary troops for a march to Skenesborough. The wounded were left at Hubbardton with a small guard commanded by Sergeant Roger Lamb of the Ninth Foot. Lamb's orders were, if attacked by the rebels, to surrender the camp and rely on the clemency of the enemy. By this time, surgeons, nurses and a small detachment of reinforcements had reached Hubbardton. Fraser's command marched the fifteen miles to Skenesborough without incident, but his soldiers were much fatigued.[142] Undoubtedly, the Scotsman was happy to see General Burgoyne, and the Englishman's feeling was mutual.

After Hubbardton, the Vermont Council of Safety, the equivalent of a state government in the newly formed independent territory, asked Warner to remain at Manchester, the town where he had ordered his men to rally, as things fell apart on the battlefield. Warner's assignment was to reorganize his Green Mountain Continental regiment and coordinate a defense of Vermont with Lieutenant Colonel Samuel Herrick, who had recently formed a ranger battalion. Their objective was to keep an eye on Riedesel, who had been ordered by Burgoyne to return to the Castleton area to squash rebel resistance and, hopefully, find recruits for the Crown. Warner's department commander, General Schuyler, ordered the Green Mountain colonel to rejoin his army in New York. Pleas from the council of safety caused Schuyler to rescind his order, and Warner remained near Manchester for defensive purposes.

In August 1777, a real threat arose when Lieutenant Colonel Friedrich Baum's expeditionary force left Burgoyne's army to gather supplies in Bennington. Warner and Herrick answered the call of Brigadier General John Stark to march to the defense of Bennington. Stark met Baum's Germans, Loyalists and Indians five miles west of Bennington on the Walloomsac River, where the irascible Stark soundly defeated Baum with assistance from both Warner and Herrick—perhaps an "ample revenge on account of the quarrel at Hubbardton."

His rugged frontier life and the physical vicissitudes of war finally took their toll on Seth Warner—and at an early age. His biographer recounts a long struggle with "complicated and distressing maladies, which he bore with uncommon fortitude and resignation, until deprived of his reason."[143] Warner died the day after Christmas in 1784 at the age of forty-two.

His adversary at Hubbardton, Simon Fraser, died a soldier's death at the equally young age of forty-eight. Following the battle at Monument Hill, Fraser rejoined Burgoyne's army at Skenesborough to begin the month-long trek to Saratoga. Fraser distinguished himself, leading his Advance Corps in the battle at Freeman's Farm on September 19 and again at what has been called the Barber wheat field fight on October 7.[144] During the latter action, Fraser was hit with a mortal wound in the abdomen, which some say was fired by an Irishman named Timothy Murphy. No matter who fired the deadly round, Burgoyne's favorite general died the next day. At his own request, the Scotsman was buried in the Great Redoubt, which

American troops depict a battle scenario at the 2014 annual reenactment at the Hubbardton Battlefield Site. Note the artillery being used by the Americans. Neither side had artillery at Hubbardton on July 7, 1777. *Author's collection.*

was part of Burgoyne's fortified line near Freeman's Farm. His burial was memorialized in the Baroness von Riedesel's campaign journal. She had accompanied her husband, General Riedesel, the man who had saved Fraser's reputation at Hubbardton.[145]

The baron himself would fight in both battles near Saratoga and was part of Burgoyne's "convention army" that surrendered to Gates on October 17, 1777. Ironically, Riedesel objected to the Bennington expedition that destroyed part of his corps and gave his Hubbardton adversary, Seth Warner, a chance to retaliate against his Germans. Unlike Burgoyne, who returned to England the following year after a short confinement in Boston, the German general stayed a prisoner until exchanged in October 1780. Riedesel's fighting days were basically over, however. He spent a brief period on Long Island and then in Quebec before returning with the baroness to Brunswick. After six years of military service under the Duke of Brunswick, he retired to his ancestral castle of Lauterbach, where he wrote his memoirs of his service in America. He died peacefully in his sleep on January 7, 1800, at the age of sixty-two.[146]

The battle of Hubbardton began with 850 British troops facing between 1,100 and 1,235 Americans. Riedesel brought 180 Germans into the fight, although his total corps in the operation amounted to about 1,100 men. Many authors who have written about Hubbardton in their campaign studies have estimated casualty numbers. There is no sense arguing the various estimates here. Numbers vary depending on the sources consulted. Williams probably has done the most thorough and accurate examination of the sources to come up with the total of killed, wounded, missing and captured on each side. He examined twenty sources to come up with the numbers he published. Williams also provided a rationale for the sources he found most credible.

In total numbers, it appears that the Americans lost 371 men at Hubbardton, while the combined British and German casualties were 208. But this gross calculation belies the heavy toll of killed and wounded on the British and German side. Drilling down on the numbers, for example, shows that 60 British and 10 Germans were killed versus 41 Americans. Another reliable reference work puts the Americans killed at 30. In terms of men wounded on both sides, the British incurred 134 wounded and the Germans 14 or a total of 148; the Americans suffered 96 wounded. The Patriots lost 234 men as prisoners to the enemy, according to Williams. Simon Fraser reported 230 prisoners taken. Burgoyne later revised this number up to 238: 1 colonel, 7 captains, 10 lieutenants and 210 rank and file. It appears that Williams may have calculated an average between Fraser's number and Burgoyne's figure. The bulk of these prisoners were the sick, disabled and unmanageable stragglers who populated the bottomland of Sucker Brook when the grenadiers came through. There were no British or German prisoners taken at Hubbardton.

As Williams pointed out: "The inadequacy of American records following the Battle and the nature of the American retreat make an accurate statement of the American killed and wounded virtually impossible." It also makes the number of Patriot missing difficult to estimate. Beyond the killed, wounded and captured, there were probably a good number of men who drifted away from their regiments during and at the close of the action. There is no point in trying to hazard a guess at this number, but it is probably safe to say that total American casualties were higher than Williams's estimates.[147]

Among the British casualties, one officer stands out, perhaps because he was the luckiest man on the field that day. The commander of Fraser's light infantry battalion, Major Alexander Lindsay, the Earl of Balcarres, was hit with "a musket ball that could have shattered his femur in his left leg," but it "glanced off a flint in his pocket and left him with only a slight flesh wound and contusion." The young earl also counted ten holes in his uniform made from shots that had missed their mark. The barrel of his officer's musket and its lock were shot off while he was holding it. "You may observe," Lindsay wrote his sister Margaret, "on this occasion I am not born to be shot whatever may be my Fate." The earl would survive the campaign but remain a prisoner of war until 1779. The remainder of his life included fathering five children, promotion to full general, governorship of Jamaica, ownership of a successful ironworks business and an inconsequential duel with Benedict Arnold, whom he had disparaged for his treason. Lindsay died at age seventy-three.

13

CONCLUSION

S imon Fraser and his redcoats, with essential help from Baron von Riedesel and his Brunswickers, won a tactical victory at Hubbardton. Despite heavy losses in terms of the percentage engaged, they had crushed the American rear guard and sent them fleeing from the battlefield. But there was no pursuit by Fraser; he had been stunningly stopped in his tracks. With no active hunt for fugitives by the British, some 67 percent of the Patriots escaped. Many of the troops who fled would see action again a month later at Bennington on August 16, a battle in which Seth Warner was again conspicuous in the American victory. Other troops would fight Fraser and Riedesel in two battles near Saratoga on September 19 and October 7, with the latter action sealing Burgoyne's fate and ending the campaign of 1777 with the surrender of Burgoyne's army on October 17.

There is little doubt that the Patriot rear guard's resistance at Hubbardton impressed the British officers who fought against them. After the battle, Ensign Thomas Hughes of the Fifty-third Foot summed up the British attitude: "This engagement did our troops the greatest honor, as the enemy was vastly superior in numbers, and it was perform'd in a thick wood, in the very style that the Americans think themselves superior to regular troops." The wounded Earl of Balcarres believed the rebels had "certainly behaved with great gallantry."[148]

How should the opposing sides be judged for their performance at Hubbardton? Contemporary reaction was generally positive. Three weeks after the battle, the *Boston Gazette* decided to reprint a letter it had from Albany dated July 14, in which the writer said, "Never did[,] nor can troops behave better than ours on this occasion. We however lost some brave officers, among whom is Col. Francis from Massachusetts. This gentleman behaved like a hero; and so did the rest of the officers." General Schuyler seemed pleased enough with the Patriots' stand at Hubbardton to send a letter to Warner asking him to "thank the troops in my name for behaving so well as you say they did at Hubbard Town."

According to Williams, "The ability of the Americans to take and hold successive positions on [the] command of their officers, particularly when all were aware that withdrawal was implicit in their mission, was impressive."[149] Warner had accomplished his mission, notwithstanding St. Clair's opinion. There was no further pursuit of the Americans by the British or Germans. Luzader came to the same conclusion, adding that Warner, Francis and their troops "displayed a disciplined courage that was rarely, if ever, surpassed during the War for Independence." He also makes the interesting observation that the Americans "seemed stronger near the end of the fight than before the engagement began—an opponent encouraged by unexpected success against brave, professionally led Regulars." Ketchum has the most interesting take on the battle. He sees it as Fraser's good luck that Warner had decided to fight at Hubbardton rather than withdraw as St. Clair's orders proscribed. Ketchum argues that if Warner had followed St. Clair into Castleton with Fraser in hot pursuit, the British brigadier might have bitten off more than he could chew in a pitched battle with the rear guard combined with the northern army. In this scenario, the British would have been outnumbered three to one.[150]

Ketchum's premise relies on the Germans continuing to move "ponderously" behind Fraser. A contrary argument could be made that Fraser could have held St. Clair and Warner in place until Riedesel came up in a Hubbardton-like maneuver that crushed the entire northern army. St. Clair's troops were tired, hungry and demoralized from their long retreat from Mount Independence. His militia units were highly unreliable. Depending on the terrain at the time of contact, British discipline, Jäger marksmanship and the bayonet might have served Fraser well.

There is little question that American fortitude and fighting spirit for several hours at Hubbardton saved St. Clair's army from a fight with Burgoyne's army. There is no guarantee, as Ketchum would have us believe, that Fraser and Riedesel would have been unable to defeat St. Clair, if the opportunity presented itself. Even if they were outnumbered against the rebels, what the British and their German reinforcements lacked in troop strength would have been made up for in aggressive leadership, discipline and tactical skill.

There is no evidence that Warner's order to withdraw to Manchester was prearranged. Most likely it was not. Warner's rear guard regiments were broken up by pressure on both flanks. The Germans created havoc with their surprise attack; the heavy and accurate firepower from the Jäger company and the threat of a bayonet charge all contributed to Warner's defeat. Acland's grenadiers and Lindsay's detachment threatened the American left. As Williams concludes, "The rear guard was withdrawing in accordance with its mission, but it must be conceded that after leaving the high log fence east of the Castleton road, military organization for the most part ceased."[151]

Williams saw the battle as a draw, although he admitted that many would see it otherwise. His rationale bears repeating in detail:

> *The British were of necessity impressed with the ability of the Americans to inflict unacceptable casualties upon them in such a brief period, and thus decisively halt the British pursuit. They remained at Hubbardton for two days after the Battle taking care of their wounded and burying their dead. Burgoyne's strategic plan to overcome St. Clair's North Army in a pincer movement between his troops at Skenesborough and the pursing troops under Fraser and Riedesel was defeated by the stand made by Warner, Francis, and Hale at Hubbardton. The Fraser-Riedesel end of the pincer remained open. It is also true that St. Clair received intelligence of the capture of Skenesborough in time to reverse course and proceed to Rutland before the Battle started. It can well be debated, however, that but for the delays inherent in the rear guard defense St. Clair might have been further along toward Skenesborough. He might not have been able to turn east to Rutland had Fraser and Riedesel defeated or by-passed Warner's troops and come up in St. Clair's rear. This was undoubtedly Burgoyne's intention.[152]*

Hubbardton was a tactical victory for the British, not a draw. The Americans were forced to leave the field—a sure sign of victory for the opposing side. Granted, Burgoyne was thwarted in his attempt to crush St. Clair in a so-called pincer movement, if that was his strategy. However, the commanding general makes no mention in his July 11 letter to Germain that this was his intent. It seems like a logical plan in hindsight, but what if he allowed Fraser to chase after the rebels because the Scotsman made it a *fait accompli*, rather than part of a grand scheme quickly devised by Burgoyne to catch St. Clair's army? And what if the best use of Fraser's corps was not available, due to the same logistical difficulties that would plague Burgoyne's army for the remainder of the campaign?

It seems evident from reading Burgoyne's letter of July 11 that he allowed Fraser to leave the main army on a mission that involved little planning. Fraser took no surgeons or medical supplies, no extra ammunition, no artillery and no food other than what the men carried in their haversacks. The condition of the Mount Independence military road would justify not taking guns; even small three- or four-pounders would have been difficult to transport. But the other items were essential to a multi-day expedition. As one historian who has studied the campaign has surmised, "Burgoyne seems to have expended little planning or consideration on the pursuit." Fraser seems to be the main culprit in these doings. As evidenced by his rush to engage the Americans as soon as he reached Sucker Brook and Monument Hill, without waiting for Riedesel, it is clear that Fraser was impetuous. He wanted to leave Mount Independence as soon as possible, and he did. There was no face-to-face meeting between the two generals to discuss a plan because Burgoyne was spending his nights aboard the *Royal George*. Most likely, Fraser traded on his friendship with Burgoyne and the confidence the commanding general had in his leadership ability. Fraser won a tactical victory—it was no draw—but the casualties suffered and time lost caused significant problems during the remainder of the campaign.[153]

There might have been a better alternative than Fraser hot-footing it through the wilderness to Hubbardton, but logistical difficulties impeded the best course of action for Burgoyne's army in the early morning hours of July 7, 1777.

An obscure German source sheds light on Burgoyne's campaign in the critical twenty-four hours after Lieutenant Twiss hauled his guns to the top of Sugar Loaf Mountain. Sometime between 1778 and 1780, an unidentified Brunswick officer penned a letter in which he outlined "Some Frank Thoughts about the Campaign of Lieutenant General John Burgoyne in 1777." The letter was more an opinion piece than a personal missive to a relative. The infantry officer served in the Printz Friedrich Regiment commanded by Lieutenant Colonel Christian Julius Pratorius, which was stationed at Fort Ticonderoga after it was captured. In the letter, the anonymous German lieutenant seeks to explain the "basic reasons for the misfortunes of this campaign, which has resulted in such negative consequences for England." He said they were "manifold." It is not the purpose here to outline the Brunswicker's entire editorial but only to highlight its pertinence to Fraser's operation.[154]

It was this officer's opinion that Burgoyne's army "would have profited greatly had it been able to take Fort George right after seizing Ticonderoga." Fort George was an unfinished fortification left over from the French and

Indian War. It was located at the southern end of Lake George. Early in the war, the Americans had seized the abandoned fort and completed it with a picketed stockade. It served as a supply depot at the head of the Lake George military road, originally built in 1755 to connect Fort Edward with the lake. Before Burgoyne invested Fort Ticonderoga, St. Clair had successfully transferred some of his stockpile of munitions and supplies to Fort George from Fort Ticonderoga and Mount Independence. He also sent his young son to Fort George shortly before Fort Ticonderoga was evacuated.[155]

The German officer claimed in his letter that Fort George "contained a vast depot of diverse provisions: ammunition, cannon, other martial necessities as well as 180 wagons with teams of four horses." The writer felt this equipment and transportation would have been useful; Burgoyne should have seized it immediately after Ticonderoga was secured. But the commanding general's own logistical support was pitiful from the start of the campaign. He lacked the means to get at least part of his army over the portage road between the Ticonderoga promontory and Lake George's northern landing. This lack of transportation prevented his army from using Lake George immediately; in the meantime, the Americans were able to cart away valuable war materiel from Fort George. Instead, "the Royal Army contented itself with pursuing the fleeing and scattered corps of General St. Clair across South Bay. [The rebels] had nothing more to lose, but they could still contest every step of the way in thickly wooded terrain," the officer said. "We gained from our victory [at Hubbardton] the advantage of taking approximately 400 prisoners, but, in exchange, we had to suffer extensive losses, particularly among the finest soldiers in the army," the German concluded. By going to Hubbardton, instead of being able to use Lake George and capturing the fort at the southern end of the lake, Burgoyne perhaps lost a great opportunity to cash in on a trove of supplies that his army would badly need in the weeks and months ahead.[156] This scenario has not been commented on by other historians of Burgoyne's campaign. It bears further investigation because if Burgoyne had had the means to use the portage road, he perhaps would not have allowed the impetuous, yet competent, Brigadier Fraser to chase after St. Clair's army and end up losing irreplaceable redcoat officers and men in western Vermont.

In the end, what happened at Hubbardton was significant for several reasons. First, Warner's decision showed he was the right commander at the time. He knew the capabilities of his troops. He also knew the area and where the best location was to make a stand. His decision to rest his men was the best one for the fatigued soldiers who had just completed a strenuous march of over twenty miles on a road that was more a foot trail than a military highway. But more importantly, Warner bought precious time for St. Clair's equally tired and perhaps demoralized army. A good understanding of the condition of St. Clair's army is found in a New Hampshire man's letter written less than two weeks after the retreat. This soldier claimed the men were "hurried at an unmerciful rate thro' the woods at the rate of thirty-five miles a day, oblidged [sic] to kill oxen belonging to the Inhabitants wherever we got them; before they were half-skinned every soldier was oblidged [sic] to take a bit & half Roast it over the fire, then before half done was oblidged [sic] to March." Once the army marched, the men were without clothes, food or drink and were "constantly wet." Even the officers, in some cases, lost their baggage and personal papers. The most telling comment this grumbling footslogger made in his letter was that St. Clair "refused to send assistance when the Cols. begged him to do it."[157]

The additional hours spent fighting at Hubbardton gave St. Clair the time he needed to move his men out of harm's way—to fight another day. And his army did fight another day when it was critically important. Allowing St. Clair the opportunity to march his army by way of Rutland, instead of Skenesborough and then to Fort Edward, was the right course of action at the time. Allowing the northern army to rally with Schuyler's forces enabled Schuyler to create a delaying strategy that sapped Burgoyne's army of its cherished foodstuffs and forage at a time when the British general's supply line was stretched back to Canada. Having enough supplies to sustain his army for several weeks at a time was absolutely essential for campaigning in the New York wilderness. It was logistics that defeated Burgoyne as much as any battlefield reverses he experienced.[158] Without an American army to implement Schuyler's delaying strategy, the Crown's battalions would have easily marched to Albany in the early fall of 1777. Warner and his delaying action at Hubbardton made Schuyler's plan possible because there was an army to carry it out.

While Fraser and Riedesel unquestionably won a tactical victory at Hubbardton, their combined loss in the battle caused irreparable damage to Burgoyne's army. It is well documented that General Carleton, the commander in chief of British forces in Canada, would not release additional reinforcements to Burgoyne. When Burgoyne captured Fort Ticonderoga, he had to detach units from his invasion force to garrison it and other installations along his route. This method, so essential to maintaining his elongated supply line, continuously reduced his army. The losses sustained at Hubbardton, therefore, were not easily accommodated. The crack troops represented by Acland's grenadier and Lindsay's light infantry battalions took casualties at Hubbardton that would seriously impair Fraser's Advance Corps as the army continued its march toward Albany.

Burgoyne, however, didn't seemed fazed by his losses, at least not at the time, or the impulsive actions of his favorite brigadier. Perhaps anticipating some criticism after the casualty lists crossed the Atlantic, Burgoyne justified Fraser's decision to bring on a fight at Hubbardton. In his preemptive report to Germain a few days after the battle, Burgoyne claimed, "The bare relation of so signal an action is sufficient for its praise." If an explanation was needed, Burgoyne continued, "It is to be considered that the Enemy might have escaped by [Fraser's] delay; that the advanced guard found themselves on a sudden too near the enemy to avoid action without retreating; and that the Brigadier had supposed the Germans were very near." As a back-handed slap at Riedesel and his German troops for taking so long to get into the fight, Burgoyne quipped, "Major General Riedesel and those he commanded pressed for a share of the glory and they arrived in time to share it."[159] Burgoyne was sticking by his man's choices—period. His remarks prefigured a growing schism in the army between the proud British regulars and their king's German hirelings. Suffice it to say, it would be a long three and a half months for General Riedesel and his Teutonic comrades.

Burgoyne's campaign would end on October 17, 1777, at Saratoga with the surrender of the Crown's army to a Patriot force under Horatio Gates. Historians have long considered Saratoga to be the turning point of the American War for Independence. This great American victory provided assurance to France that the rebels had a chance to beat Great Britain. In early 1778, France, and soon other European powers, would join the fledgling United States in an alliance to defeat Great Britain. Money, men and munitions would flow from France to the former British colonies. For the Americans, the goal of independence was secured by the surrender of another British army at Yorktown, Virginia, four years nearly to the day after Burgoyne's capitulation at Saratoga. But the seeds of victory at Saratoga were sown in the fields and hills around Hubbardton, Vermont, on a hot July day in 1777. With St. Clair's army saved and Burgoyne's elite corps crippled, it is an inescapable conclusion that Warner's stand at Hubbardton might have been the rear guard action that saved America.

NOTES

Preface

1. The more popularly known battle of Bennington (a town situated in Vermont) was actually fought in New York State on the Walloomsac River near Hoosick Falls on August 16, 1777.
2. Both quotes are found in Elting, *Battles of Saratoga*, 32.
3. Williams, *Battle of Hubbardton*, 1–44.
4. Information about Hubbardton's chronological evolution into a state historic site is found on its website: http://historicsites.vermont.gov/directory/hubbardton.

Introduction

5. Weddle, "'Change of Both Men and Measures,'" 837–38. Weddle believes the story of King George's reaction might be apocryphal.
6. Estimates of Burgoyne's army vary from 7,400 to 9,500 depending on which account is read. Charles Snell, a Saratoga Park historian, has done the most comprehensive analysis of troop data available for the campaign. Snell, "Report on the Strength," 87. Burgoyne himself claims his army's strength on July 1, 1777, was 7,390. In later testimony from his deputy adjutant general, Lieutenant Colonel Robert Kingston, this number changes to 7,631 for returns on July 1. See Burgoyne, *State of the Expedition*, 12, 97. For a discussion of the use

of German troops in America, see Baer, "Britain's Decision to Hire," 45–50. For the quality of Burgoyne's army, see Hargrove, *General John Burgoyne*, 268.

7. Burgoyne's *Thoughts for Conducting the War from the Side of Canada*, dated February 28, 1777, is reprinted in Cubbison, *Burgoyne and the Saratoga Campaign*, 178–86. St. Leger would hold the temporary or local rank of brigadier for the campaign.

8. Burgoyne, *State of the Expedition*, 39.

CHAPTER 1

9. Baxter, *British Invasion*, 204; Fraser, "General Fraser's Account," 143; Kendall, "William Twiss: Royal Engineer," 175–76. Twiss would end his military career in 1825 as a full general.

10. Cubbison, *Burgoyne and the Saratoga Campaign*, 268–69.

11. Davis, *Where a Man Can Go*, 65.

12. Elting, *Battles of Saratoga*, 31.

13. Fraser was lieutenant colonel of the Twenty-fourth Regiment of Foot but held the temporary or local rank of brigadier for this campaign. While Fraser would act as a brigadier general under Burgoyne, his proper title in the eighteenth-century British army was brigadier, not brigadier general. This rank is commonly referred to as general by historians and will be used the same way in this narrative as well.

14. The Hampshire Grants was disputed territory mutually claimed by New Hampshire and New York until Vermont declared its independence from both states in January 1777.

15. Van Tyne, *War of Independence*, 373.

16. Furneaux, *Battle of Saratoga*, 58. Gates felt at least 13,600 men were needed.

17. St. Clair, *Narrative of the Manner*, 244–45.

18. Hadden, *Journal Kept in Canada*, 81–82.

19. Cubbison, *Burgoyne and the Saratoga Campaign*, 272; Fraser, "General Fraser's Account," 147; Nickerson, *Turning Point of the Revolution*, 116–17.

20. In eighteenth-century military terminology, the terms regiment and battalion are often used interchangeably to describe the same type of unit. Grant was a veteran of the French and Indian War. Reference to Grant's career and rank is found in Hadden, *Journal Kept in Canada*, 210–11.

21. Seven of Fraser's grenadier and light infantry companies were from regiments serving in Burgoyne's army during the campaign, and three grenadier and light infantry companies came from regiments left in Canada under Carleton.

22. Hadden, *Journal Kept in Canada*, 83.

23. Ibid., 82; Fraser, "General Fraser's Account," 143; Stanley, *For Want of a Horse*, 107–08. Stanley speculates that the officer diarist was in the Forty-seventh Foot.

24. Fraser, "General Fraser's Account," 142.

25. Wheeler and Wheeler, *Mount Independence–Hubbardton*, 88–115; Crown Point Road Association, *Historical Markers*, 1–11.

26. Ketchum, *Saratoga: Turning Point*, 116–17; Wheeler and Wheeler, *Mount Independence–Hubbardton*, 103–08.

27. *Proceedings of a General Court Martial*, 35.

28. Ibid., 6, 11.

29. Fitzpatrick, *Writings of George Washington*, 253–55, 271, 273–77, 331–33, 357, 376, 378, 380.

Chapter 2

30. *Proceedings of a General Court Martial*, 35.

31. Ibid., 4, 22–3, 46.

32. Wickman, "Breakfast on Chocolate," 497.

33. Baxter, *British Invasion*, 205.

34. Ketchum, *Saratoga: Turning Point*, 116–17.

35. *Proceedings of a General Court Martial*, 11.

36. Gerlach, "Fall of Ticonderoga," 148.

37. Fraser, "General Fraser's Account," 144; Baxter, *British Invasion*, 208; Doblin, *Eyewitness Account*, 59.

38. Elting, *Battles of Saratoga*, 31–34; Ketchum, *Saratoga: Turning Point*, 177–81.

39. *Proceedings of a General Court Martial*, 26–27, 35–36.

40. Jackman, *With Burgoyne from Quebec*, 138–39; *Proceedings of a General Court Martial*, 29; Nickerson, *Turning Point of the Revolution*, 146–47; Ketchum, *Saratoga: Turning Point*, 184; Duling, "Thomas Anburey," 1–14. Anburey's identity and even rank is questionable. An appendix in Hadden written by Horatio Rogers says Anburey served as a volunteer in the grenadier company of the Twenty-ninth Foot. Hadden, *Journal Kept in Canada*, 491.

41. Hadden, *Journal Kept in Canada*, 486.

42. Riedesel claims that he captured Mount Independence: "Riedesel immediately embarked his men and took possession of Fort Independence, at the same time that General Fraser occupied Fort Carillon [i.e. Fort Ticonderoga]." Stone, *Memoirs, and Letters and Journals*, vol. 1, 113.

43. Fraser, "General Fraser's Account," 144; Doblin, *Specht Journal*, 53; Doblin, *Eyewitness Account*, 59; Retzer, "Journal of the Hessen-Hanau," 42.

CHAPTER 3

44. Cubbison, *Burgoyne and the Saratoga Campaign*, 269.

45. Wheeler and Wheeler, *Mount Independence–Hubbardton*, 107.

46. Cubbison, *Burgoyne and the Saratoga Campaign*, 270.

47. Ibid.

48. Ibid.; Cubbison, *"Artillery Never Gained,"* 81–86; Hadden, *Journal Kept in Canada*, 89.

49. Doblin, *Specht Journal*, 54.

50. Stone, *Memoirs, and Letters and Journals*, vol. 1, 114.

51. Snell, "Report on the Strength," 65–66.

52. Cubbison, *Burgoyne and the Saratoga Campaign*, 271; Francis's chaplain is quoted in Hadden, *Journal Kept in Canada*, 86.

53. Lossing, *Pictorial Field-Book*, vol. 1, 144. According to Amos Churchill, Hubbardton's nine families were headed by Benjamin Hickok, Uriah Hickok, William Turbridge, Samuel Churchill, Jesse Churchill, John Selleck, Abdial Webster, Benjamin Boardman and William Spaulding. See Henry Hall, "The Battle of Hubbardton," typescript circa 1877, John Williams Papers, MS 149, Vermont Historical Society, Special Collections, Montpelier, VT, 16 (hereafter VHS).

54. Hall, "Battle of Hubbardton," 16; Ketchum, *Saratoga: Turning Point*, 207–09; Folsom, "Battle of Hubbardton," 17.

55. Williams, *Battle of Hubbardton*, 9.

56. The name of this mountain varies depending on the mapmaker's preference. For purposes of this book, the maps and text refer to the mountain as Mount Zion, the locally accepted modern name. Today, Mount Zion has several marked hiking trails, and a climb to the top provides a wonderful view of the Hubbardton battlefield and contiguous terrain.

57. Barker and Huey, *1776–1777 Northern Campaigns*, 59, 126–27. Barker and Huey note in their book that the Faden-produced map of Hubbardton includes the wrong given name initial for Gerlach.

58. *Proceedings of a General Court Martial*, 37.

59. Williams, *Battle of Hubbardton*, 60. Williams's analysis concludes that St. Clair "had moved on before Francis and his rear guard came up. Most of Francis's Eleventh Massachusetts Continental Regiment was thus with St. Clair, only two of his companies having been selected for the rear guard." Williams further concludes, "Francis' rear guard fought as it had marched, augmented by Warner's depleted regiment and encumbered by Hale's invalids, sick, stragglers and intoxicated, attached to Captain Carr's company."

60. *Proceedings of a General Court Martial*, 36–37; Williams, *Battle of Hubbardton*, 9, 46.

61. Chipman, *Life of Colonel Seth Warner*, iii, 35, 41–43; Malone, *Dictionary of American Biography*, 468.

62. Nickerson, *Turning Point of the Revolution*, 148.

63. Ebenezer Fletcher, *The Narrative* (n.p.: privately printed, 1813). See John Williams Papers, MS 149, VHS.

64. *Proceedings of a General Court Martial*, 36–37.

65. Ibid., 37, 47.

66. Williams, *Battle of Hubbardton*, 10–12; Hadden, *Journal Kept in Canada*, 483–85.

67. Elting, *Battles of Saratoga*, 32. Elting flatly claims, "St. Clair's colonels failed him," a rather unfair charge considering that Warner and his subordinates had a good defense position and stood toe to toe with the British regulars for several hours at Hubbardton. This writer does not have much sympathy for the stragglers that Warner had to deal with on July 6. As Elting sarcastically observes, "There were several hundred stragglers who—after the immemorial habit of that breed—would have been clamorous against the injustice of having to get up and go on." This statement leaves the unspoken impression that Warner should have shot the stragglers and disabled men who failed to move out on the afternoon of July 6. Warner was not going to do this, and it is obvious why he did not.

68. Williams, *Battle of Hubbardton*, 12; John Clement, "Notes and Narrative on the History of the Battle circa 1960," John Williams Papers, MS 149, VHS; Stone, "Captain Enos Stone's Journal," 8.

69. Williams, *Battle of Hubbardton*, 13; Clement, "Notes and Narrative on the History of the Battle circa 1960," 2–3.

70. Fraser, "General Fraser's Account," 144.

71. Ibid., 144–45.

72. Baxter, *British Invasion*, 209.

73. Fraser, "General Fraser's Account," 145; Cubbison, *Burgoyne and the Saratoga Campaign*, 202.

74. The term "Jäger" is used as both a singular and plural noun like the word "deer." The alternate spelling "Jeager" is pronounced the same way. E-mail explanation from Eric Schneitzer, park historian, Saratoga National Historical Park, Stillwater, New York, to the author, dated May 5, 2014. For background on the organizational origins of the Jäger, see Boatner, *Encyclopedia of the American Revolution*, 549. Boatner uses "s" to pluralize Jäger, which is incorrect. For background on Jäger tactics and weaponry, see Barker and Huey, "Military Jaegers, Their Civilian Background and Weaponry," 1–15. Barker and Huey's article also uses "s" to pluralize Jäger.

75. Fraser, "General Fraser's Account," 145; Stone, *Memoirs, and Letters and Journals*, vol. 1, 114.
76. Fraser, "General Fraser's Account," 145; Stone, *Memoirs, and Letters and Journals*, vol. 1, 114.
77. Fraser, "General Fraser's Account," 145. The officer is named in Hill's account on page 18.
78. Ibid.

CHAPTER 4

79. Ibid.; Williams, *Battle of Hubbardton*, 16.
80. Williams, *Battle of Hubbardton*, 16; Fraser, "General Fraser's Account," 146; Hadden, *Journal Kept in Canada*, 500.
81. Moses Greenleaf Diary, John Williams Papers, MS 149, VHS. Captain Enos Stone recorded in his journal that the Americans were detained until "7am: then appeared the Enemy in Sight." Stone, "Captain Enos Stone's Journal," 8. Stone's mention of being detained probably refers to Warner waiting for his reconnaissance party to return from north. He had sent out two hundred men in search of British Loyalists and Indians who were heard to be raiding nearby settlements.
82. Gerlach, "Fall of Ticonderoga," 151–52; Williams, *Battle of Hubbardton*, 21, 24, 60; Wright, *Continental Army*, 198, 212, 320.
83. Hall, "Battle of Hubbardton," 16, 18. In his unpublished typescript, Hall claims to have interviewed Joseph Bird for this account.
84. Napier, "Lord Francis Napier's Journal," 300; Baxter, *British Invasion*, 209.
85. Hall, "Battle of Hubbardton," 18; Lossing, *Pictorial Field-Book*, vol. 1, 145; Wheeler and Wheeler, *Mount Independence–Hubbardton*, 223.
86. Williams, *Battle of Hubbardton*, 20.
87. Fletcher, *Narrative*, 2.
88. Williams, *Battle of Hubbardton*, 20.
89. Ibid., 33.
90. Fraser, "General Fraser's Account," 145; Jackman, *With Burgoyne from Quebec*, 140; Duling, "Thomas Anburey," 6–12.

CHAPTER 5

91. Fraser, "General Fraser's Account," 145; Baxter, *British Invasion*, 209.
92. Jackman, *With Burgoyne from Quebec*, 145, 209; Hadden, *Journal Kept in Canada*, 88.
93. Moses Greenleaf Diary.
94. Napier, "Lord Francis Napier's Journal," 300; Fraser, "General Fraser's Account," 145.
95. Baxter, *British Invasion*, vi, 209–10. Lieutenant Digby served in Captain Wight's grenadier company.
96. Fraser, "General Fraser's Account," 145–46; Baxter, *British Invasion*, 210. The Earl of Balcarres is quoted in Elting, *Battles of Saratoga*, 32.
97. Jackman, *With Burgoyne from Quebec*, 141; Duling, "Thomas Anburey," 7. Both Ketchum and Luzader include the clubbed musket story in their campaign histories.

CHAPTER 6

98. No one interested in the study of Hubbardton should fail to consult Ennis Duling's article, cited previously, for a discussion of how original sources might contain plagiarized elements from other sources. Duling, "Thomas Anburey," 1–14.
99. Nickerson, *Turning Point of the Revolution*, 150–51; R. Ernest Dupuy, "The Battle of Hubbardton: A Critical Analysis," unpublished typescript, John Williams Papers, MS 149, VHS; Duling, "Thomas Anburey," 8–9.
100. Duling, "Thomas Anburey," 9–10.
101. Ketchum, *Saratoga: Turning Point*, 201–02.
102. Morrissey, *Saratoga 1777: Turning Point*, 35–37.
103. Luzader, *Saratoga: A Military History*, 64–65; Logusz, *With Musket & Tomahawk*, 123–24; Corbett, *No Turning Point*, 129–32.
104. Duling, "Thomas Anburey," 8–9. After a number of visits to the battlefield and discussions with Carl Fuller, who has been the site manager at Hubbardton for many years, I came to the same conclusion as Duling. Mount Zion is too high and too far away to be a factor in the battle. It makes no sense to have the British grenadiers climb up and down Mount Zion. They accomplished their goal without going near the mountain.

Chapter 7

105. Williams, *Battle of Hubbardton*, 20.
106. Fraser, "General Fraser's Account," 146–47.
107. Williams, *Battle of Hubbardton*, 25.
108. Cubbison, *Burgoyne and the Saratoga Campaign*, 271.
109. Stanley, *For Want of a Horse*, 111.

Chapter 8

110. Williams, *Battle of Hubbardton*, 29.
111. Fraser, "General Fraser's Account," 146.
112. Hall, "Battle of Hubbardton," 19–20. Hall quoted Ethan Allen's comments without any notation of where they were from originally.
113. Randall, *Ethan Allen*, 260, 356–57.
114. Baxter, *British Invasion*, 210.
115. *Proceedings of a General Court Martial*, 37.
116. Ibid. For Dunn's version, which is similar but less detailed, see ibid., 36.
117. Ibid.
118. Baxter, *British Invasion*, 210; Pell, "Diary of Joshua Pell," 8–9; Burgoyne's order is quoted in Riedesel's *Memoirs*. Stone, *Memoirs, and Letters and Journals*, vol. 1, 118.
119. Hall, "Battle of Hubbardton," 20; Williams, *Battle of Hubbardton*, 29.
120. Fraser, "General Fraser's Account," 146.

Chapter 9

121. Stone, *Memoirs, and Letters and Journals*, vol. 1, 115.
122. Ibid. See Williams, *Battle of Hubbardton*, 38, for the time of day.
123. Stone, *Memoirs, and Letters and Journals*, vol. 1, 115.
124. Ibid.; Jackman, *With Burgoyne from Quebec*, 141.
125. Fraser, "General Fraser's Account," 146; Stone, *Memoirs, and Letters and Journals*, vol. 1, 115–16. The letter from the German grenadier is found in Hall, "Battle of Hubbardton," 24, without any source information. Benjamin Titcomb's wound is certified in a document dated April 8, 1784, in the Fort Ticonderoga Collection with a copy on file in the Saratoga National Historical Park library.

Chapter 10

126. Jackman, *With Burgoyne from Quebec*, 140, 142; Williams, *Battle of Hubbardton*, 30; Hall, "Battle of Hubbardton," 26–27; Chipman, *Life of Colonel Seth Warner*, 80; Stone, *Memoirs, and Letters and Journals*, vol. 1, 116; Doblin, *Specht Journal*, 55; Baxter, *British Invasion*, 211–12; Stanley, *For Want of a Horse*, 111. One of Bird's quotes used in Hall's article specifically refers to the "ridge of Pittsford mountain," so Bird knew it as a geographical location. When he is recalling incidents about Francis's death, he does not refer to a ridge, mountain or Pittsford by name but only uses the term "hill." This might have confused Williams. When Bird uses the term "hill," it seems logical that he is referring to Monument Hill rather than Pittsford "mountain."

Chapter 11

127. Baxter, *British Invasion*, 212–13.

128. Hall, "Battle of Hubbardton," 25–26; Baxter, *British Invasion*, 210.

129. Hadden, *Journal Kept in Canada*, 495; Warner's quote is in Elting, *Battles of Saratoga*, 32. Elting estimates that about five hundred retreated over Pittsford Ridge when Warner gave the order.

130. Hall, "Battle of Hubbardton," 27.

131. Jackman, *With Burgoyne from Quebec*, 142, 146; Cubbison, *Burgoyne and the Saratoga Campaign*, 115–24.

132. Hadden, *Journal Kept in Canada*, 88.

133. An appendix in Hadden's journal indicates the following: "The seventy Americans captured by the stratagem of the British officer with fifteen men, can, we think, refer only to Col. Nathan Hale and a part of the Second New Hampshire Regiment; for no considerable number of the Americans surrendered in a body on the retreat from Hubbardton, other than he and a portion of his battalion." Ibid., 483.

134. Allen, *Narrative of Colonel Ethan*, 106. For a speculative defense of Colonel Hale's conduct at Hubbardton without any specific primary source evidence, see Hadden, *Journal Kept in Canada*, 483–504.

135. Lossing, *Pictorial Field-Book*, vol. 1, 145.

136. Hadden, *Journal Kept in Canada*, 489.

Chapter 12

137. See ibid., 88 for a list of sixteen officers who were killed or wounded and their regimental affiliation.

138. Fraser, "General Fraser's Account," 146; Baxter, *British Invasion*, 213.

139. Stone, *Memoirs, and Letters and Journals*, vol. 1, 117.

140. Fraser, "General Fraser's Account," 146; Baxter, *British Invasion*, 217.

141. Baxter, *British Invasion*, 212, 219–20; Fraser, "General Fraser's Account," 146–47.

142. Fraser, "General Fraser's Account," 146–47.

143. Chipman, *Life of Colonel Seth Warner*, 83.

144. Recently it was determined by Saratoga National Historical Park staff that the Barber family did not own the wheat field at the time of the battle. Signage at that location will be changed to reflect this new interpretation.

145. Boatner, *Encyclopedia of the American Revolution*, 397.

146. Ibid., 933–34.

147. Williams, *Battle of Hubbardton*, 43–44, 65; Fraser, "General Fraser's Account," 146; Cubbison, *Burgoyne and the Saratoga Campaign*, 272; Peckham, *Toll of Independence*, 37.

Chapter 13

148. Ensign Hughes is quoted in Corbett, *No Turning Point*, 132; Balcarres is quoted in Elting, *Battles of Saratoga*, 32.

149. The *Boston Gazette* and Schuyler are quoted in Hadden, *Journal Kept in Canada*, 494.

150. Williams, *Battle of Hubbardton*, 43; Luzader, *Saratoga: A Military History*, 65; Ketchum, *Saratoga: Turning Point*, 215.

151. Williams, *Battle of Hubbardton*, 43.

152. Ibid., 83.

153. Cubbison, *Burgoyne and the Saratoga Campaign*, 65, 270–73.

154. Barker, "British Invasion of New York," 1–2.

155. Ibid., 3.

156. Ibid.

157. Hadden, *Journal Kept in Canada*, 487.

158. For a detailed discussion of Burgoyne's logistical problems and the effect they had on his campaign, see Cubbison, *Burgoyne and the Saratoga Campaign*, 19–145.

159. Ibid., 272.

BIBLIOGRAPHY

Primary Sources

Allen, Ethan. *Narrative of Colonel Ethan Allen's Captivity*. Burlington, VT: Chauncey Goodrich, 1846.

Barker, Thomas M. "The British Invasion of New York as Seen by a Braunschweig Subaltern at Fort Ticonderoga: 'Some Frank Thoughts About the Campaign of Lieutenant General John Burgoyne in 1777.'" *Journal of the Johannes Schwalm Historical Association* 7, no. 1 (2001): 1–11.

Baxter, James Phinney. *The British Invasion from the North: The Campaigns of Generals Carleton and Burgoyne from Canada, 1776–1777, with the Journal of Lieut. William Digby, of the 53rd, or Shropshire Regiment of Foot*. Albany, NY: Joel Munsell's Sons, 1887.

Burgoyne, John. *A State of the Expedition from Canada as Laid before the House of Commons by Lieutenant-General Burgoyne….* 2nd ed. 1780. Reprint, New York: Arno Press, 1969.

Cubbison, Douglas R. *Burgoyne and the Saratoga Campaign: His Papers*. Norman, OK: Arthur H. Clark Company, 2012.

Doblin, Helga, trans. *The American Revolution, Garrison Life in French Canada and New York: Journal of the Officer in the Prinz Friedrich Regiment, 1776–1783*. Westport, CT: Greenwood Press, 1993.

———. *An Eyewitness Account of the American Revolution and New England Life: The Journal of J.F. Wasmus, German Company Surgeon, 1776–1783*. New York: Greenwood Press, 1990.

———. *The Specht Journal: A Military Journal of the Burgoyne Campaign*. Westport, CT: Greenwood Press, 1995.

Fitzpatrick, John C., ed. *The Writings of George Washington*. 39 vols. Washington, D.C.: United States Government Printing Office, 1933.

Fraser, Simon. "General Fraser's Account of Burgoyne's Campaign and the Battle of Hubbardton: A Letter to John Robinson Dated 13 July, 1777." *Proceedings of the Vermont Historical Society* 4 (1898–1902).

Hadden, Lieutant James M. *A Journal Kept in Canada and Upon Burgoyne's Campaign in 1776 and 1777*. With an explanatory chapter and notes by Horatio Rogers. 1884. Reprint, Whitefish, MT: Kessinger, n.d.

Jackman, Sydney, ed. *With Burgoyne from Quebec: An Account of the Life at Quebec and of the Famous Battle at Saratoga by Thomas Anburey*. Toronto: Macmillan of Canada, 1963.

Napier, Lord Francis. "Lord Francis Napier's Journal of the Burgoyne Campaign." *Maryland Historical Society Magazine* 57, no. 4 (December 1962): 300–04.

Pell, Joshua, Jr. "Diary of Joshua Pell, Jr.: An Officer of the British Army in America, 1776–1777." *Bulletin of the Fort Ticonderoga Museum* 1 (July 1929).

Proceedings of a General Court Martial, Held at White Plains, in the State of New-York by Order of His Excellency General Washington, for the Trial of Major General St. Clair, August 25, 1778. Philadelphia: Hall and Sellers, 1778.

Retzer, Henry J., trans. "Journal of the Hessen-Hanau Erzprinz Infantry Regiment: June to August 1777 Kept by Chaplain Philipp Theobald." *Journal of Johannes Schwalm Historical Association* 7, no. 1 (2001): 40–42.

Stanley, George F.G., ed. *For Want of a Horse: A Journal of the Campaigns Against the Americans in 1776 and 1777 Conducted from Canada, by an Officer Who Served with Lieutenant General Burgoyne*. Sackville, NB: Tribune Press Limited, 1961.

St. Clair, Arthur. *Narrative of the Manner in Which the Campaign Against the Indians, in the Year One Thousand Seven Hundred and Ninety Was Conducted, Under the Command of Major General St. Clair*. Philadelphia: Jane Aitken Printer, 1812.

Stone, Enos. "Captain Enos Stone's Journal." *New England Historical and Genealogical Register* 15 (October 1861).

Stone, William L., ed. *Memoirs, Letters and Journals of Major General Riedesel During His Residence in America.* 2 vols. Albany, NY: J. Munsell, 1868.

Wickman, Donald H., ed. "Breakfast on Chocolate: The Diary of Moses Greenleaf, 1777." *The Bulletin of the Fort Ticonderoga Museum* 15, no. 6 (1997): 482–506.

Williams, John. John Williams Papers, MS 149. Montpelier, VT: Special Collections, Vermont Historical Society.

SECONDARY SOURCES

Baer, Friederike. "Britain's Decision to Hire German Troops in the War for American Independence." *Journal of the Johannes Schwalm Association* 15, (2012): 45–50.

Barker, Thomas M., and Paul R. Huey. "Military Jaegers, Their Civilian Background and Weaponry." *Journal of the Johannes Schwalm Historical Association* 15 (2012): 1–15.

———. *The 1776–1777 Northern Campaign of the American War for Independence and Their Sequel: Contemporary Maps of Mainly German Origin.* Fleischmanns, NY: Purple Mountain Press, 2010.

Boatner, Mark M., III. *Encyclopedia of the American Revolution.* 3rd edition. Mechanicsburg, PA: Stackpole Books, 1994.

Chipman, Daniel. *The Life of Colonel Seth Warner, with an Account of the Controversy Between New York and Vermont, from 1763 to 1775.* Burlington, VT: C. Goodrich and Company, 1858.

Corbett, Theodore. *No Turning Point: The Saratoga Campaign in Perspective.* Norman: University of Oklahoma Press, 2012.

Crown Point Road Association. *Historical Markers on the Crown Point Road: A Touring Guide.* Rutland, VT: Sharp and Company, 2011 Edition.

Cubbison, Douglas R. *"The Artillery Never Gained More Honour": The British Artillery in the 1776 Valcour Island and 1777 Saratoga Campaigns.* Fleischmanns, NY: Purple Mountain Press, 2007.

Davis, Robert P. *Where a Man Can Go: Major General William Phillips, British Royal Artillery, 1731–1781.* Westport, CT: Greenwood Press, 1999.

Duling, Ennis. "Thomas Anburey at the Battle of Hubbardton: How a Fraudulent Source Misled Historians." *Vermont History* 78, no. 1 (Winter/Spring 2010): 1–14.

Elting, John R. *The Battles of Saratoga*. Monmouth Beach, NJ: Philip Freneau Press, 1977.

Folsom, William R. "The Battle of Hubbardton." *Vermont Quarterly* 20, (1952): 3–18.

Furneaux, Rupert. *The Battle of Saratoga*. New York: Stein and Day, 1971.

Gerlach, Don R. "The Fall of Ticonderoga in 1777: Who Was Responsible." *The Bulletin of the Fort Ticonderoga Museum* 14, no. 3 (Summer 1982): 131–57.

Hargrove, Richard J., Jr. *General John Burgoyne*. Newark: University of Delaware Press, 1983.

Kendall, John Charles. "William Twiss: Royal Engineer." *Duquesne Review* 15, no. 1 (Spring 1970): 175–91.

Ketchum, Richard M. *Saratoga: Turning Point of America's Revolutionary War*. New York: Henry Holt and Company, 1997.

Logusz, Michael O. *With Musket & Tomahawk: The Saratoga Campaign and the Wilderness War of 1777*. Havertown, PA: Casemate, 2010.

Lossing, Benson J. *The Pictorial Field-Book of the Revolution*. 3 vols. New York: Harper and Brothers, 1850, 2008 reprint.

Luzader, John F. *Saratoga: A Military History of the Decisive Campaign of the American Revolution*. New York: Savas Beatie, 2008.

Malone, Dumas, ed. *Dictionary of American Biography*. 22 vols. New York: Charles Scribner's Sons, 1928–1958.

Morrissey, Brendan. *Saratoga 1777: Turning Point of a Revolution*. New York: Osprey, 2000.

Nickerson, Hoffman. *The Turning Point of the Revolution or Burgoyne in America*. Cranbury, NJ: Scholar's Bookshelf, 2005 reprint.

Peckham, Howard H. *The Toll of Independence: Engagements and Battle Casualties of the American Revolution*. Chicago: University of Chicago Press, 1974.

Randall, Willard Sterne. *Ethan Allen: His Life and Times*. New York: W.W. Norton Company, 2011.

Schnitzer, Eric. Email to the author dated May 5, 2014.

Snell, Charles W. "A Report on the Strength of the British Army under Lieutenant General John Burgoyne, July 1, to October 17, 1777 and on the Organization of the British Army on September 19 and October 7, 1777." Stillwater, NY: Saratoga National Historical Park, February 28, 1951.

Van Tyne, Claude. *The War of Independence*. Boston: Houghton Mifflin Company, 1929.

Weddle, Kevin J. "'A Change of Both Men and Measures': British Reassessment of Military Strategy after Saratoga, 1777–1778." *The Journal of Military History* 77, no. 3 (July 2013): 837–65.

Wheeler, Joseph L., and Mabel A. Wheeler. *The Mount Independence–Hubbardton 1776 Military Road*. Benson, VT: J.L. Wheeler, 1968.

Williams, John. *The Battle of Hubbardton: The American Rebels Stem the Tide*. Montpelier: Vermont Division for Historic Preservation, 1988.

Wright, Robert K., Jr. *The Continental Army*. Washington, D.C.: Center for Military History, United States Army, U.S. Government Printing Office, 1982.

INDEX

ABOUT THE AUTHOR

D r. Bruce M. Venter is president of America's History, LLC, a tour and conference company that offers tours of Revolutionary War battlefields and historic sites. The company annually holds a nationally recognized conference on the American Revolution in Williamsburg, Virginia. He serves as first vice-president of the American Revolution Round Table of Richmond. An article on Burgoyne's campaign appeared in *Patriots of the American Revolution* magazine. His forthcoming book entitled *Kill Jeff Davis: Union Raid on Richmond* will be published by the University of Oklahoma Press in 2015. Venter holds a bachelor's degree in history from Manhattan College and master's and doctoral degrees from the University at Albany. The Venters' summer home on Lake George is only fifty miles from the Hubbardton Battlefield Site.